MURRAY N. ROTHBARD VS. THE PHILOSOPHERS

UNPUBLISHED WRITINGS ON HAYEK, MISES, STRAUSS, AND POLANYI

Murray N. Rothbard vs. the Philosophers

Unpublished Writings on Hayek, Mises, Strauss, and Polanyi

Edited with an Introduction and Notes
by Roberta A. Modugno

LvMI

LUDWIG VON MISES

Ludwig von Mises Institute
518 West Magnolia Avenue
Auburn, Alabama 36832
mises.org

Large Print Edition published 2012 by Skyler J. Collins.
Visit: www.skylerjcollins.com

Cover image by StockFreeImages.com.

ISBN-13: 978-1479372362
ISBN-10: 1479372366

Contents

PREFACE

ROBERTA MODUGNO HAS IN HER scholarly career made a habit of "getting there first." She wrote the first book in any language on the thought of Murray Rothbard, *Murray N. Rothbard e l'anarco-capitalismo americano*, published by Rubbettino in 1998, and she also is the author of the first Italian book on Mary Wollstonecraft's political thought. In the present book, she has once more led the way.

Murray Rothbard was a prolific scholar, as a mere glance at his bibliography will disclose. But his published books and articles, even including those that have appeared posthumously, do not exhaust his scholarly contributions. When he died in January 1995, he left his papers and correspondence to the Mises Institute. The most important of these papers, from the point of view of libertarian scholarship, consist of reports he wrote when he worked for the William Volker Fund. In these reports, Rothbard commented on a wide variety of subjects, including economics, history, political theory, philosophy, sociology, and anthropology. Like Terence, Rothbard could say, "Nothing human is alien to me." These reports often provide more details of his views on particular points than are available from his published books; in some cases, these reports raise altogether new issues.

It is Roberta Modugno's great merit to have been the first scholar to make some of this material available to the public. After she gained access to the unpublished papers, she published (also with Rubbettino) a selection of them, translated into Italian, in 2005. The present book is the first publication of these papers in their original English.

Besides the papers, the book includes Professor Modugno's scholarly introduction, which stresses Rothbard's relations to the thought of Leo Strauss and Friedrich von Hayek. In addition, she has provided detailed explanatory notes to the selections.

Even experienced students of Rothbard will learn much from this book. His criticism of social Darwinism in the first selection is of classic stature; and he makes a searching criticism of Hayek on the rule of law. In his discussion of Caroline Robbins, his amazing depth of scholarship is present in full force. Although Robbins had just completed the first comprehensive study of British classical liberalism in the eighteenth century, Rothbard was able to correct and add to her findings.

The nine selections published here form only a small sample of the unpublished papers; future books will make many more of them available. But Roberta Modugno was there first.

David Gordon
Ludwig von Mises Institute

Introduction

Law and Nature in the Work of Murray N. Rothbard

Rothbard's Unpublished Writings

In 1952, Murray Rothbard received a grant from the William Volker Fund to write a book on Austrian economics, based on the ideas of Ludwig von Mises, to be used as a textbook for university economics courses. That book became *Man, Economy, and State*, published some ten years later. It contained an in-depth investigation of Austrian economics and its policy implications, and it went far beyond the standard university textbook. In the same year of 1952, Rothbard, now aged 26, began to work for the Volker Fund as a senior analyst, and over a period of about ten years he reviewed books, journals, articles, and manuscripts in search of intellectual allies with libertarian leanings. Rothbard enjoyed this kind of work as it offered him the opportunity to read, extremely rapidly, countless books by many different authors. This was a period of hard work, but it was also a time of intellectual development and growth.

The Volker Fund was founded in 1932 by a Kansas City entrepreneur, William Volker. Later, Volker's nephew, Harold Luhnow, was responsible for the fund's consolidation and development in the 1940s and '50s. This foundation played a crucial role in supporting and disseminating the work of Hayek, who was writing *The Constitution of Liberty*, and the work of many other libertarian scholars both at the University of Chicago and elsewhere. It organized conferences and seminars at prestigious universities and was one of the most influential classical-liberal foundations in the United States.

Since the end of the 1940s, Rothbard had also been working part time as a consultant to the National Book Foundation (a subsidiary of the Volker Fund) and for the Foundation for Economic Education. The Foundation for Economic Education (FEE) was founded by Leonard E. Read in 1946, with headquarters in a mansion on the banks of the Hudson River in New York. Its aim was to disseminate libertarian ideas, especially in the area of economics. Rothbard first made contact with this foundation when he requested a copy of a pamphlet against rent control, *Roofs or Ceilings?* written by Milton Friedman and George Stigler. The young Rothbard had attended Stigler's economics lectures at Columbia University.

The reviews and comments published in the following pages date from the years when Rothbard was working for the Volker Fund, and the two classical-liberal foundations, National Book Foundation, and FEE. Given their nature, they comprise a set of writings that are very heterogeneous, composed in a style that is sometimes informal and marked by the biting irony that was to become a typical feature of Rothbard's prose. In them, one can find some of the major themes that characterize the thought of the author.

These writings are published here for the first time, in their original English, and the decision to publish them was made for various reasons. Some pieces clarify the author's position in relation to intellectuals such as Leo Strauss and Karl Polanyi on subjects such as progress, technology, and on what today is termed "globalization." Others, such as the two sets of comments on Hayek's *Constitution of Liberty*, contain not only the criticisms—later found in *Ethics of Liberty*—of the Hayekian concept of "coercion," but also some interesting criticisms of the rule of law as a guarantee of liberty and of the absence of references to natural law in Hayek's work. Furthermore, these writings help shed light on the genesis of Rothbard's thought. His criticisms of Hayek's and Mises's ideas date back to 1958 and 1960 respectively; and it is actually here that, for the first time, Rothbard thoroughly and extensively expresses his dissent from the ideas of the two great masters. The criticisms of Mises are the same as those contained in *Ethics of Liberty*, but the comments on the Symposium on Relativism of 1960 mark the first time that Rothbard distances himself from some Misesian positions. This is an interesting set of documents showing how the main lines of Rothbardian thought were already firmly in place between the late 1950s and the early 1960s as regards subjects such as the possibility of absolute ethical values based on natural law, the nonaggression axiom, and the criticism of the state.

But that is not all. As early as 1948, we find in the comments made by the twenty-two-year-old Rothbard on Cutten's paper, "Rugged Individualism," arguments that demolish the aberrant theories of social Darwinism, revealing that the young author's individualism was already mature before he met Mises. Allusions to the immorality of the state's initiatives for social welfare and criticisms of the state were a sign that the development of Rothbard's thought already included the idea of the state as aggressor.

Alongside these writings, there are very positive comments on Lionel Robbins's *The Great Depression* and on Caroline Robbins's *The Eighteenth-Century Commonwealthman*. The volume by Lionel Robbins is presented as "one of the great economic works of our time."[1] Robbins attributes responsibility for the Wall Street Crash of 1929 to the interventionist economic policies that caused the expansion of credit in the preceding years. After this, recovery was slow because of policies that interfered with the capacity of the market to correct the structure of production that had been damaged by the preceding expansion of credit, thereby increasing the length and the severity of the Depression.

---

[1]Murray N. Rothbard, "Review of Lionel Robbins, *The Great Depression*" (London: Macmillan, 1937); see p. 79 in this volume.

Rothbard also greatly appreciates Caroline Robbins's monumental work on the eighteenth-century republicans. He considers the principal merit of her work to be that it fills the gap between the Glorious Revolution of 1688 and the liberal and republican ideas that emerged at the end of the eighteenth century, thus rediscovering a whole series of liberal, radical, dissident, and republican thinkers. Personalities like Thomas Gordon and John Trenchard—the authors of the famous *Cato's Letters*—Thomas Hollis, John Burgh, and Francis Hutcheson are restored to historiography, underlining their important role in preserving and developing the English liberal and libertarian tradition.

ROTHBARD AND LEO STRAUSS

ONE OF THE BASIC themes of the writings presented here is the possibility of a rational foundation for ethical values. Another is Rothbard's constant reference to natural law and natural rights. Because of these themes, the writings on Strauss, although brief, are important. Rothbard is always critical of Leo Strauss but he agrees with him on the need for a rational basis for ethics and absolute values. These positions are seen both in the review of *What is Political Philosophy?* and in the comments on Strauss's paper for the Symposium on Relativism (organized by the Volker Fund in 1960). According to Rothbard, the great virtue of Strauss's work "is that he is on the forefront of the fight to restore and resurrect *political philosophy* from the interment given it by modern positivists and adherents of scientism—in short, that he wants to restore values and political ethics to the study of politics." However, Rothbard thinks that Strauss's work also contains an important flaw:

The great defect is that Strauss, while favoring what he considers to be the classical and Christian concepts of natural law, is bitterly opposed to the seventeenth- and eighteenth-century conceptions of Locke and the rationalists, particularly to their "abstract," "deductive" championing of the natural rights of the individual: liberty, property, etc.

Strauss, in fact, has been the leading champion, along with Russell Kirk and the Catholic scholars in America, of a recent trend in Locke historiography . . . to sunder completely the "bad," individualist, natural-rights type natural law of the seventeenth and eighteenth centuries, from the "good" classical-Christian type—good, presumably, because it was so vague and so "prudential" that it offered very little chance to defend individual liberty against the state. In this reading, Hobbes and Locke are the great villains in the alleged perversion of natural law.

To my mind, this "perversion" was a healthy sharpening and development of the concept. My quarrel with Strauss, Kirk, et al., therefore, is not only valuational—that they are anti-natural rights and liberty, and I am for them—but also factual and historical: for they think that the Lockeans had an entirely different concept of natural law, whereas I think that the difference—while clearly there—was a sharpening development, rather than a perversion or a diametric opposite.[2]

This is where Rothbard's criticism of the Straussian concept of modern natural law first appears.[3] Strauss argues

---

[2]Murray N. Rothbard, "Letter on *What is Political Philosophy?* by Leo Strauss"; see p. 91 in this volume.

[3]This theme comes up in later works. See, for example, Murray N. Rothbard, *An Austrian Perspective on the History of Economic Thought, vol. 1, Economic Thought Before Adam Smith* (Cheltenham, U.K.: Eward Elgar, 1995), pp. 313–14, 339.

that modern natural law is a degeneration of the classical natural law that is an expression of civic virtue. In Strauss's view, the individualism of the Lockean tradition, with its theory of property, breaks with the classical and Scholastic tradition and represents a decline from the values of the past, placing the individual and his rights at the center of the universe with consequences such as "the solution of the political problem through economic means," of which he disapproves.[4] Strauss writes that

> Locke's teaching on property, and therewith his whole political philosophy, are revolutionary not only with regard to the biblical tradition but with regard to the philosophic tradition as well. Through the shift of emphasis from natural duties or obligations to natural rights, the individual, the ego, had become the center and origin of the moral world, since man—as distinguished from man's end—had become that center or origin.[5]

Safeguarding the individual's right to property becomes an aim of the kind of politics that had ceased to draw inspiration from a natural end, wisdom, and virtue.

Rothbard sees Strauss as an icon of conservatism, pressing an invitation to return to the ancients, and as a critic of a modernity heralding the historicism and relativism that led to the impossibility of making judgments of binding value for the whole community. Affirming that values are subjective and, above all, can change with the times would make it

---

[4]Leo Strauss, *What Is Political Philosophy? And Other Studies* (Glencoe, Ill.: Free Press of Glencoe, 1959), p. 49. At the heart of Strauss's idea is the critical reconstruction of modernity as a break with the ancient and medieval politico-philosophical tradition. See also Shadia B. Drury, *The Political Ideas of Leo Strauss* (New York: St. Martin's Press, 1988); Raimondo Cubeddu, *Leo Strauss e la filosofia politica moderna* (Naples: ESI, 1983).

[5]Leo Strauss, *Natural Right and History* (Chicago: University of Chicago Press, [1953] 1965), p. 248.

impossible to pronounce any judgment on political regimes. Indeed, it should be recalled that Strauss is trying to restart the search for the best regime and a just society at a moment in history when Europe was being torn apart by Nazism. He is thus trying to find an answer to the "Western moral and political crisis" and to relaunch political philosophy, that is, "the attempt truly to know both the nature of political things, and the right, or good, political order."[6] In this light, the essay *On Tyranny* seems to take a stand against tyranny—an absolute evil. With his analysis of *Hiero* by Xenophon and his condemnation of the lack of any distinction between the king and the tyrant in Machiavelli's work, Strauss is trying to show a way of warding off the dangers of tyranny. In this case, therefore, Rothbard's comments regarding *On Tyranny* seem overly severe. By claiming not only the possibility but also the right to pass value judgments, Strauss is railing against value-free modern political science. Strauss maintains that

> the new political scientist as pure spectator is not committed to any value; in particular, he is neutral in the conflict between liberal democracy and its enemies. . . . One is thus led to wonder whether the distinction between facts and values, or the assertion that no Ought can be derived from an Is, is well founded. . . . We conclude that the "relativism" accepted by the new political science according to which values are nothing but objects of desire is based on an insufficient analysis of the Is . . . and furthermore that one's opinion regarding the character of the Is settles one's opinion regarding the character of the Ought. . . . At any rate, if a man is of the opinion that as a matter of fact all desires are of equal dignity, since we know of no factual consideration which would entitle us to assign different dignities to different desires,

---

[6]Strauss, *What is Political Philosophy?* p. 12. See also Raimondo Cubeddu, Giovanni Giorgini, and Flavia Monceri, "Leo Strauss sui diritti naturali e il liberalismo," *Élites* 2 (2004): 118–24.

> he cannot but be of the opinion . . . . that all
> desires ought to be treated as equal within the
> limit of the possible, and this opinion is what is
> meant by permissive egalitarianism.[7]

In both *What is Political Philosophy?* and *Thoughts on Machiavelli*, Strauss criticizes modern thinkers and defends classical political philosophy. For the ancients, virtue rather than liberty is the true end of political life, and political philosophy is driven by the search for the best political order. And so, for Strauss, Machiavelli becomes the evil genius of modernity, challenging the ancient Christian teachings and freeing political reality from morality.

Concerning the Straussian conception, Rothbard questions the thesis that identified the modern theory of natural rights as a break with the past. He places more emphasis on continuity with the past rather than on a sharp division. According to the continuity thesis, individual natural rights derive from natural law. Rothbard underlines the Scholastic, Thomist, and Christian roots of the Lockean doctrine of natural rights. In the individualism of modern natural rights theory, Rothbard finds not a corruption but an enrichment of the natural law tradition, and the beginning of a new way to understand human means and political ends. Thus, while Rothbard appreciates the Straussian idea of natural law as a battle against the prevailing relativism of values, he is unable to accept Strauss's invitation to his readers to reclaim "the classic natural right doctrine in its original form" that, "if fully developed, is identical with the doctrine of the best regime."[8]

Rothbard cites Alessandro Passerin d'Entrèves in support of the theory that there was a link between Thomism and the Grotian development in the doctrine of natural law and writes that according to Passerin d'Entrèves the:

---

[7]Leo Strauss, *Liberalism, Ancient and Modern* (Ithaca, N.Y.: Cornell University Press, 1989; New York: Basic Books, 1968), pp. 220–22.

[8]Strauss, *Natural Right and History*, p. 144.

definition of natural law has nothing revolutionary. When he maintains that natural law is that body of rules which man is able to discover by the use of his reason, he does nothing but restate the Scholastic notion of a rational foundation of ethics. Indeed, his aim is rather to restore that notion which had been shaken by the extreme Augustinianism of certain Protestant currents of thought. When he declares that these rules are valid in themselves, independently of the fact that God willed them, he repeats an assertion which had already been made by some of the Schoolmen. . . .

Grotius's aim, D'Entrèves adds, "was to construct a system of laws which would carry conviction in an age in which theological controversy was gradually losing the power to do so." Grotius and his juristic successors—Pufendorf, Burlamaqui, and Vattel—proceeded to elaborate this independent body of natural law in a purely secular context, in accordance with their own particular interests, which were not, in contrast to the Schoolmen, primarily theological.[9]

In *An Austrian Perspective on the History of Economic Thought* Rothbard states,

we should realize that the scholastics may have dominated medieval and post-medieval traditions,

---

[9]Murray N. Rothbard, *The Ethics of Liberty* (Atlantic Highlands, N.J.: Humanities Press, 1982), p. 5. The reference is to Alessandro Passerin d'Entrèves, *La dottrina del diritto naturale* (Milan: Edizioni di Comunità, 1954), pp. 51–52. It has recently been pointed out that the continuity between natural law and natural rights in the thought of Passerin d'Entrèves probably refers more to the function historically carried out by natural law rather than to a doctrinal continuity. See Raimondo Cubeddu, "La concezione del diritto naturale in Alessandro Passerin d'Entrèves," in *Alessandro Passerin d'Entrèves pensatore europeo*, edited by Sergio Noto (Bologna: Il Mulino, 2004), pp. 179–210.

but that despite this fact, they were pioneers and
elaborators of the natural law *and* natural rights
traditions. The pitting of "tradition" versus
"modernity" is largely an artificial antithesis. . . .
Locke may have been and indeed was an ardent
Protestant, but he was also a Protestant scholastic, heavily influenced by the founder of Protestant
scholasticism, the Dutchman Hugo Grotius, who in
turn was heavily influenced by the late Spanish
Catholic scholastics. . . . While Locke developed
libertarian natural rights thought more fully than
his predecessors, it was still squarely embedded in
the scholastic natural law tradition.[10]

Within this vision, the Rothbardian idea of a link
between the laws of nature and natural rights becomes less
distinct at the point where the author emphasizes the
enrichment brought by the Levellers and Locke in terms of
individualism. Rothbard says that while Aristotle's vision of
man led to the state being seen as the place of the good and
virtuous action, "it was, in contrast, the Levellers and John
Locke in seventeenth-century England who transformed
classical natural law into a theory grounded on methodological and hence political individualism."[11] The continuity thesis has recently been corroborated by the work of Brian
Tierney who clearly questions the ideas of Strauss and
Michel Villey on the contrast between an ancient Aristotelian doctrine of natural law and a modern theory of
subjective individual rights.[12] While for Villey the modern

---

[10]Rothbard, *An Austrian Perspective*, vol. 1, pp. 313–14.

[11]Rothbard, *The Ethics of Liberty*, p. 21.

[12]See Strauss, *Natural Right and History*; Michel Villey, *La for-
mation de la pensée juridique moderne* (Paris: Editions
Montchrestien, 1975); and Brian Tierney, *The Idea of Natural
Rights: Studies on Natural Rights, Natural Law, and Church Law,
1150–1625* (Atlanta, Ga.: Scholars Press, 1997). See also Annabel
S. Brett, *Liberty, Right, and Nature: Individual Rights in Later
Scholastic Thought* (Cambridge: Cambridge University Press, 1997).

theory of subjective rights has its roots in the nominalist philosophy of Ockham, Tierney identifies the concept of *ius* as a subjective right in the writings of the twelfth-century canonists. John Finnis and Germain Grisez also follow the continuity line, but they are really more Kantians than true Thomists.[13] In point of fact, Finnis and Grisez integrate natural law with a deontological theory—with elements deriving from Kant.[14]

While not forgetting the many different positions taken by today's supporters of the theory of natural rights, Rothbard can be counted among those who, like Henry Veatch, base natural rights on the Aristotelian/Thomist theory of natural law.[15] However, Rothbard's position is particularly original for two reasons: first, because from the concept of self-ownership, he deduces the axiom of nonaggression, the true cornerstone of the Rothbardian system, which he views as a clarification of the classic triad of the natural rights to life, liberty, and property;[16] second, because of the extreme conclusions that Rothbard arrives at regarding natural law and the role of the state. In fact, Rothbard wants "to establish an objective ethics which affirms the overriding value of liberty, and morally condemns all forms of statism."[17]

The theme of the rational foundation of ethics and absolute values becomes predominant in Rothbard's comments on the Symposium on Relativism organized by the

---

[13]John Finnis, *Natural Law and Natural Rights* (Oxford: Clarendon, 1980).

[14]Henry B. Veatch, *Human Rights: Fact or Fancy?* (Baton Rouge: Louisiana State University Press, 1985), p. 104.

[15]For an examination of these distinctions, see Raimondo Cubeddu, "Legge naturale o diritti naturali? Alcune questioni di filosofia politica liberale," *Quaderni dell'Istituto Acton* 15 (2004).

[16]It seems that Rothbard owes this idea to Ayn Rand. Cf. Ayn Rand, "Man's Rights," in *The Virtue of Selfishness* (New York: Signet, 1964).

[17]Rothbard, *The Ethics of Liberty*, p. 213.

Volker Fund. The conference, held in 1960, witnessed a contrast between Mises and Leoni on one side, and Strauss on the other.[18] Obviously, in this case, Rothbard sides with Strauss. From the time of his *Prefatory Note*, Rothbard makes it clear he is in favor of absolute values:

> The absolutist believes that man's mind, employing reason . . . is capable of discovering and knowing truth: including the truth about reality, and the truth about what is best for man and best for himself as an individual.
>
> The relativist denies this, denies that man's reason is capable of knowing truth, and does so by claiming that rather than being absolute, truth is relative to something else. . . . Philosophically, I believe that libertarianism—and the wider creed of sound individualism of which libertarianism is a part—must rest on absolutism and deny relativism.[19]

This represents a clear—and apparently definitive—division within the Austrian School of economics, with Hayek and the Hayekians on one side and many of the American disciples of the School (among whom are libertarians *à la* Rothbard) on the other. The concept of natural law is in some ways extraneous to the Austrian School of economics, which favors an evolutionary conception of institutions and law following the approach of Menger and Hayek.

---

[18]The conference papers were published in H. Schoeck and J.W. Wiggins, eds., *Relativism and the Study of Man* (Princeton, N.J.: D. Van Nostrand, 1961).

[19]Rothbard, "The Symposium on Relativism: A Critique"; see p. 103 in this volume.

CRITICISM OF THE SUBJECTIVISM OF VALUES

THE CRITICISM OF MISES is paradigmatic. Rothbard distances himself from the praxeological and value-free defense of the free market that Mises proposes, and instead supports the need for political philosophy to find universally valid basic values for life in society. Mises bases his own liberalism on the subjectivity of values and ends, but for Rothbard this makes Mises an "ethical relativist;" and, in his opinion, ethical relativism is the "great defect in this paper."

> What I have been trying to say is that Mises's utilitarian, relativist approach to ethics is not nearly enough to establish a full case for liberty. It must be supplemented by an absolutist ethic—an ethic of liberty, as well as of other values needed for the health and development of the individual— grounded on natural law, i.e., discovery of the laws of man's nature. Failure to recognize this is the greatest flaw in Mises's philosophical worldview.[20]

The *subjectivism* of ends and values, and the defense of the free market from a praxeological point of view are correct procedures in the context of praxeology, but they do not satisfy the Rothbardian need for ethics to have a rational basis. Praxeology, the science of human action, tells us that the free-market economy is the best way of achieving the widest possible well-being and the whole variety of human ends—ends that are subjective, as are the values that underlie them. The subjectivity of values and ends is the nodal point of Misesian thought and the basis for an open society. Mises follows Hume's assumption that it is impossible to derive values from facts. Since the economy is concerned with facts, it cannot have any direct implications for ethics. For Mises, value judgments merely express preferences of a

---

[20]Ibid., p. 103 in this volume.

subjective nature that could be considered neither true nor false. Rothbard disagrees with this view of ethics; one problem he sees with it is that it appeals only to subjective values to convince others that the best social system is the market economy. Mises thinks that the choice of the free market should be based on the consequences of such a preference. While not denying that value judgments are the expression of essentially subjective choices, Mises thinks that practically any informed person would choose the free market. In contrast, Rothbard holds that certain facts regarding human nature will produce objective judgments about what is best for man. Moreover, Rothbard does not consider Mises's main arguments regarding capitalism fully satisfactory. Mises's attempt to found capitalism on a subjective basis, albeit valid as far as it goes, requires a further supporting argument.

Rothbard is one of those authors who maintains that, in practice, few of our judgments are "pure" in the sense required by the facts-values dichotomy. Although it is not possible to derive prescriptive statements from facts, we can derive them from judgments on facts. This is Strauss and Philippa Foot's position.[21] Besides this, in Rothbard's opinion, there are self-evident truths able to provide a basis for an objective ethics. The ownership of oneself, of one's own body, is an example of such a truth. Mises rejects this position; and according to his way of thinking, criteria for objectively evaluating value judgments do not exist:

> The ultimate end of action is always the satisfaction of some desires of the acting man. Since nobody is in a position to substitute his own value judgments for those of the acting individual, it is vain to pass judgment on other people's aims and volitions. No man is qualified to declare what

---

[21]See Strauss, *Natural Right and History* (Los Angeles and Berkeley: University of California Press, 1978); Philippa Foot, *Virtues and Vices* (Oxford: Blackwell, 1978) and *Natural Goodness* (Oxford: Clarendon Press, 2001).

would make another man happier or less discontented.[22]

Given his ethical subjectivism, Mises rejects the entire notion of natural law.

> The teachings of utilitarian philosophy and classical economics have nothing at all to do with the doctrine of natural right. . . . They recommend popular government, private property, tolerance, and freedom not because they are natural and just, but because they are beneficial.[23]

Why does Rothbard resort to an argument of an ethical nature to support the free market? He must, after all, have been aware that the question of natural law is extremely controversial. Rothbard explains that Mises's way of proceeding is correct in relation to praxeology, but it is nevertheless unable to tell us what is best for the human being. In brief, Mises's reasoning does not satisfy the Rothbardian requirement of establishing an objective and rational basis for liberty. Mises shows that policies constraining the market economy would lead to undesired consequences for almost all people. Once this has been demonstrated, everyone should logically accept the market economy. Rothbard points out that the situation is not quite so simple, since some individuals could actually desire consequences such as shortages of goods, hunger, or poverty to occur. Alternatively, some could have a short-term interest in favoring heavily interventionist policies; others could be egalitarian

---

[22]Ludwig von Mises, *Human Action: A Treatise on Economics*, scholar's edition (Auburn, Ala.: Ludwig von Mises Institute, 1998), pp. 18–19.

[23]Mises, *Human Action*, p. 174. On the different positions of Mises and Rothbard on these questions, see David Gordon, "Le implicazioni etiche e politiche della Scuola austriaca di economia," in David Gordon and Roberta A. Modugno, eds., *Individualismo metodologico: dalla Scuola austriaca all'anarco-capitalismo* (Rome: Luiss Edizioni, 2001), pp. 36–71.

even to the point of preferring equal poverty for all; still others could be nihilistic and desire a scarcity of goods or could complain about the excessive well-being of our society and its waste of resources. Some might have a short-term interest linked to interventionist policies and desire positions of power within the bureaucracy. These various possibilities contradict Mises's conviction that all supporters of state intervention will become supporters of the free market once they have grasped the logical consequences of a reduction in market freedom.

Rothbard's intention is to make his own argumentation in support of freedom more persuasive.[24] Anyone who understands all the benefits to be derived from the free market—well-being, peace, and cooperation—and is still against it, must address an argument of an ethical nature. According to Rothbard, this would be an objective and rational argument. He finds in natural law a guide to enable us to understand what are the best ends for man, i.e., what ends are in accordance with human nature. He writes, "The natural law . . . elucidates what is best for man—what ends man should pursue that are most harmonious with, and best tend to fulfill, his nature."[25]

The Aristotelian/Thomist formulation of the idea of a natural law plays a very important role in Rothbard's theory, which takes up the idea of an order of natural laws that can be uncovered by reasoning:

---

[24]In *Power and Market* Rothbard expresses some uncertainties about a position attempting to defend freedom solely on the basis of value-free positions—an attempt lacking any persuasive force for those who intend to impose their own values by coercion and who persist in their intentions even when they have been shown the probable disastrous economic consequences of abandoning the free-market economy. See *Power and Market* (Menlo Park, Calif.: Institute for Humane Studies, 1970), p. 209.

[25]Rothbard, *The Ethics of Liberty*, p. 10.

> In the Thomistic tradition, natural law is ethical as well as physical law; and the instrument by which man apprehends such law is his reason. . . . Aquinas, then, realized that men always act purposively, but also went beyond this to argue that ends can also be apprehended by reason as either objectively good or bad for man.[26]

Rothbard also reproaches Bruno Leoni regarding ethical relativism because Leoni was "scornful of the very idea that ethical values *should* be rationally demonstrated," while "values should be demonstrated because reason is the only sure, solid ground of conviction about values."[27] Again, when reviewing *Freedom and the Law* by Leoni, Rothbard criticizes Leoni's theory because it lacks a standard on which to judge the content of laws that had evolved over time. It is not enough to affirm the existence of a spontaneous process from which customs and institutions developed; it is necessary to subject them to the strict test of reason in order to judge their conformity or otherwise with individual freedom on the basis of an objective ethical standard.[28]

Rothbard, contra Mises, thinks it possible to deduce ethical principles from certain facts regarding human nature. He maintains that

> Individual human beings are not born or fashioned with fully formed knowledge, values, goals, or personalities; they must each form their own values and goals, develop their personalities, and learn about themselves and the world around them. Every man must have freedom, must have the scope to form, test, and act upon his own choices, for any sort of development of his own

---

[26]Ibid., p. 5.

[27]Rothbard, "The Symposium on Relativism: A Critique"; see p. 103 in this volume.

[28]Murray N. Rothbard, "On Freedom and the Law," *New Individualist Review* 1, no. 4 (1962): 37–40.

personality to take place. He must, in short, be
free in order that he may be fully human.[29]

Rothbard's formulation seems, at its heart, to be very
close to the so-called Veatch School in that it is characterized by the rehabilitation of Aristotelian/Thomist metaphysics for the foundation of natural law and the consequent
anchoring of natural rights.[30] Furthermore, even when Rothbard follows a deductive, axiomatic approach — beginning
with the axiom of human action, which is considered a self-
evident truth — this truth is founded on the nature of man,
thus placing it in an Aristotelian/Thomist context, as
opposed to the Kantian context in which the *a priori* truth of
human action would be considered a consequence of the logical structure of the human mind.[31] Instead, Rothbard
derives the right of self-ownership from natural law, rather
than considering it an axiom, since it is in harmony with
what is supposed to be the natural end of the human being—
the promotion of his own survival.

While the starting points for Rothbard and Veatch are
very similar, the two authors differ profoundly as regards the
concept of the common good and the role of the state.
Veatch thinks that the state should be an instrument, the
institutional framework by means of which all the rights of
life, freedom, and ownership could be guaranteed, in order
that each person can realize himself as a human being, i.e.,
realize the end that is in accordance with man's nature. The
concept of the common good is therefore strictly bound to

---

[29]Murray N. Rothbard, *The Logic of Action II: Applications and
Criticism from the Austrian School* (Cheltenham, U.K.: Edward
Elgar, 1997), pp. 3–4. Originally prepared for the Symposium on
Human Differentiation, for the Institute of Paper Chemistry in
Appleton, Wisconsin, 1970, and sponsored by the Institute for
Humane Studies.

[30]See Veatch, *Human Rights*.

[31] Murray N. Rothbard, "In Defense of 'Extreme Apriorism'," in
The Logic of Action I: Method, Money and the Austrian School
(Cheltenham, U.K.: Edward Elgar, 1997), pp. 105–06.

this conception. The common good means that group of institutions allowing citizens within the *polis* to enjoy the necessary conditions for *the good life* or, rather, to live as human nature requires.[32] For Rothbard, on the other hand, the concept of the justice of private property makes any kind of taxation—and therefore the state—unacceptable.

There are also profound differences with Passerin d'Entrèves, whom Rothbard quotes in support to the theory of the continuity between natural law and natural rights. He obviously does not agree with him regarding the conception of the state. The question of the relationship between Veatch and libertarianism merits further examination. In fact, as regards the idea of the common good not as an end in itself but rather as an instrument or an intermediate objective, Veatch declares his own intellectual debt to Douglas Den Uyl and Douglas Rasmussen. What is more, in *Human Rights: Fact or Fancy?* besides thanking the libertarians, he recognizes the stimulus and support he received from Den Uyl, Rasmussen, and Rothbard.[33]

Although he says he is not a libertarian, Veatch clearly appreciates the support of the libertarians for individual rights and "their determination to find a proper philosophical justification for such rights."[34] However, when Veatch goes on to consider the libertarian basis for individual rights, he seems to examine only one particular version of libertarian ethics, defined as ethical or rational egoism. According to rational egoism, the consequences of a lack of respect for agreed rights and obligations is so serious that everyone should consider it in his own personal interest to conform to the rules guaranteeing the respect of individual rights. Veatch writes, "rational individualism . . . is often associated with present-day libertarianism."[35] While, on the one hand,

---

[32] Veatch, *Human Rights*, p. 122.

[33] Ibid., p. ix.

[34] Ibid.

[35] Ibid., p. 39.

it is possible to recognize the merits of rational egoism (in contrast to utilitarian ethics) in not sacrificing individual rights to the objective of the greatest happiness for the greatest number; on the other hand, Veatch thinks that "an ethics that is erected entirely upon considerations of rational self-interest is not really an ethics at all." He further criticizes this type of libertarian ethics when he writes,

> [W]ho can ever honestly believe that human beings can, by and large, be persuaded . . . to recognize that it is in their own interest to respect the rights of others to life, liberty, property, and all the rest; and that, seeing that such moral and law abiding behavior is in their own interest, they will then act accordingly? All of this seems, alas, highly unlikely.[36]

In this way, Veatch reclaims and relaunchs the idea of anchoring natural rights in Aristotelian/Thomist metaphysics. What seems strange is that Veatch makes no reference whatsoever to Rothbard's *Ethics of Liberty*, even though he recognizes that rational egoism is by no means the only form that libertarian ethics can assume. He also affirms that "libertarianism" is not a univocal term but one that encompasses various different strands of moral philosophy.[37] Rothbard follows a similar path to that of Veatch, founding natural law and natural rights on Aristotelian/Thomist metaphysics; and he demonstrates that he has taken up Veatch's suggestions, to which he makes references on several occasions.[38] However, there

---

[36]Ibid., p. 46.

[37]Veatch does, however, include Rothbard's volume in the bibliography.

[38]In *Ethics of Liberty*, Rothbard quotes the following works by Veatch: *For an Ontology of Morals: A Critique of Contemporary Ethical Theory* (Evanston, Ill.: Northwestern University Press, 1971) and *Rational Man: A Modern Interpretation of Aristotelian Ethics* (Bloomington: University of Indiana Press, 1962).

seems to have been a more explicit and direct relationship between Henry Veatch and Den Uyl and Rasmussen, who were even closer philosophically to Veatch than Rothbard had been.

CRITICISM OF HAYEK:
HISTORICAL RIGHTS AND NATURAL RIGHTS

ROTHBARD'S CRITICISM OF HAYEK'S formulation, both evolutionist and fallibilist, is closely connected to the discussion of natural law. The fact that Hayekian and Rothbardian premises are irreconcilable emerges in the two reviews of *Constitution of Liberty*. To explain the reasons for liberty, Hayek starts from evolutionary and fallibilist positions that are inevitably going to contrast with the doctrine of natural law and rationalism, the latter being the premises for Rothbard's anarcho-capitalist theory. In Rothbard's opinion, one of the shortcomings of Hayek's work is that he totally ignores the tradition of natural law, even when discussing theorists who were actually great supporters of the doctrine of natural law, as in the case of John Locke. Hayek seems to be unaware of this great tradition of thought, which played such an important role in the growth of liberal ideas, in safeguarding the intangible individual sphere, and in limiting the powers of the state—and which, we should not forget, contributed so much to the history of constitutionalism itself, given the links between natural rights, contractualism, and constitutionalism.[39]

---

[39]On the historical role of the notion of natural law, see Passerin d'Entrèves, La dottrina del diritto naturale, and Guido Fassò, La legge della ragione (Milan: Giuffrè, 1999).

As it happens, this subject is more complex than first appears. We have to bear in mind that Hayek uses evolutionary premises as a starting point for his thinking about the rule of law and law in general. It represents one of the greatest expressions of the tradition of spontaneous order developed by Adam Smith and Adam Ferguson in the Scottish Enlightenment and which, continued by Edmund Burke, led to Friedrich Carl von Savigny, Henry Maine, and Carl Menger and the Austrian School of economics. In Hayek's work, the fundamental concept, and one of his most original ideas, is that of cultural evolution, which has to do with the origin and development of institutions such as religion, law, the market, and, in general, self-generating and self-regulating systems that shape a complex society. In this sense, for Hayek, rights are certainly not *natural*; but, given that they have evolved spontaneously, they cannot be termed *artificial* either.

A starting point in Hayek's thought is the false dichotomy between *natural and artificial*, the latter term identifying the product of an intended project. This dichotomy obstructs the correct understanding of the process of cultural evolution that produced our traditions and our civilization. There is, however, an intermediate category of phenomena resulting from human action but not from human planning. Following the reasoning of the late Scholastics, the Spanish Jesuits who used the term *naturalis* to indicate social phenomena that had evolved over time,[40] Hayekian teaching explains that "In this sense, our traditional, spontaneously evolved morals are perfectly natural rather than artificial, and it would seem fitting to call such traditional rules 'natural laws'."[41]

In other words, something is natural if it has evolved spontaneously over time. What is important is to go beyond the

---

[40]This particular reference is to Louis de Molina. See F.A. Hayek, *Law, Legislation, and Liberty*, 2 vols. (London: Routledge, 1982).

[41]F.A. Hayek, *The Fatal Conceit* (London: Routledge, 1988), p. 143.

false dichotomy that, by considering anything driven by a conscious plan as artificial and anything with instinctive characteristics as natural, brings us inevitably to a rationalist constructivism. This is why Hayek deplores the fact that the early signs of an evolutionist model to explain society have been abandoned in favor of a different conception of natural law understood as rationalist law, a law according to reason.[42]

---

[42]The term rationalism indicates an attitude of unshakeable faith in the creative capacities of human reason in the field of social and political institutions. This attitude leads to the belief that any institution and any order are the result of an intended and conscious plan, in the belief that reason can control and plan everything that man does. Hayek writes that "human institutions are made by man. Though in a sense man-made, i.e., entirely the result of human actions, they may yet not be designed, not be the intended product of these actions." Constructivism consists in "the belief that since all 'institutions' have been made by man, we must have complete power to refashion them in any way we desire." See F.A. Hayek, *The Counter-Revolution of Science: Studies in the Abuse of Reason* (Glencoe, Ill.: The Free Press, 1952). The "spontaneous order" school of thought maintains that a large part of human institutions did not necessarily derive from a mind that planned and directed them, i.e., institutions, law, and customs are the result of human action but not the result of a human plan; rather, they are the consequences of spontaneous collaboration among individuals. This is the great theme found in Bernard de Mandeville, David Hume, Adam Ferguson, Adam Smith, and Edmund Burke, right up to the main exponents of the Austrian School of economics, Menger, Mises, and Hayek. It was in fact Hayek who, on the basis of a different attitude to constructivist rationalism, introduced the categories of true and false individualism into the history of liberal thought. True individualism highlights the limits and the fallibility of human reason, while false individualism holds that reason is able to plan everything and leads to the claim of infallible social engineering. See F.A. Hayek's "Individualism: True and False" in *Individualism and Economic Order* (London: Routledge and Kegan Paul, 1949). Awareness of the limits to reason and to all that rationality could intentionally achieve in the field of political and social institutions, and thus the impossibility of a totally rational way of acting in the Cartesian sense, derives from the inevitable limitations of our knowledge. In other words, it would not be possible to have total knowledge of all the relevant facts regarding social structure and human activities. As Hayek

These are the theoretical premises that led Hayek to question some entrenched views in the history of political institutions. First and foremost is the idea that a normative system has been intentionally created by someone or is the result of an explicit agreement. For Hayek, both the assumption that a right is the fruit of the famous Bodinian sovereignty—the power to make and break laws—and the contractualist assumption are only the result of a constructivist rationalism that stands in the way of a correct understanding of the evolution of political and social institutions. It is a short step to the criticism of legal positivism, which, in fact,

> proves on examination to be entirely based on what we have called the constructivist fallacy. It is

---

explains, "A designer or an engineer needs all the data and full power to control or manipulate them if he is to organize the material objects to produce the intended result. But the success of action in society depends on more particular facts than anyone can possibly know." It is important to remember "the necessary and irremediable ignorance on everyone's part of the particular facts which determine the actions of all the several members of human society" (F.A. Hayek, *Law, Legislation, and Liberty*, vol. 1, *Rules and Order* [London: Routledge, 1973], p. 29). Scattered and fallible knowledge encourages holding both the gradualism and the experience of the past in high esteem. Awareness of the existence of the inevitable, unintentional consequences of intentional human actions leads to severe criticism of rationalism or constructivism. Criticism of the constructivist presumption is further extended by Karl R. Popper. Popperian epistemology—claiming that the study of society necessarily depends on one's perspective, as is the case when studying any subject—explains that infallible social engineering is impossible. Popper makes a distinction between utopian social engineering and step-by-step mechanics: "The piecemeal engineer knows, like Socrates, how little he knows. He knows that we can learn only from our mistakes. Accordingly, he will make his way, step by step, carefully comparing the results expected with the results achieved, and always on the look-out for the unavoidable unwanted consequences of any reform." See Karl Popper, *The Poverty of Historicism* (Boston: Beacon Press, 1957), p. 67. On this subject, see also Dario Antiseri, *Liberi perché fallibili* (Soveria Mannelli: Rubbettino, 1995) and *Trattato di metodologia delle scienze sociali* (Turin: UTET, 2000).

actually one of the main offshoots of that rationalist constructivism which, in taking literally the
expression that man has "made" all his culture
and institutions, has been driven to the fiction
that all law is the product of somebody's will.[43]

In the field of law, Hayek wants to rehabilitate the evolutionist teachings of Edward Coke and Matthew Hale, in
stark contrast with Thomas Hobbes or, in more recent
times, with Hans Kelsen. This is how things like *jus gen-
tium*, mercantile law, the customary laws practiced at fairs,
and common law took the form of a *cosmos*, that is, of a
spontaneous order that made use of the knowledge scattered among different individuals, and in which no single
mind had a planning or coordinating role. Following Nicola
Matteucci's ideas, it is therefore possible to conceive a
Hayekian position that is not in direct contrast with the concept of natural law, understood, obviously, in terms of cultural evolution. Matteucci underlines the fact that for Coke
and the English jurists, there was no contrast between natural law and common law, because the latter was simply the
implementation of the natural law principles from which it
developed historically over the centuries and with the con-
sensus of many generations.[44]

It is precisely in this sense that Edward Coke was able to
write that the common law expressed the "perfection of reason . . . because by many successions of ages it hath been
fined and refined by an infinite number of grave and learned
men, and by long experience growne to a such perfection."[45]

---

[43]Hayek, *Law, Legislation, and Liberty*, vol. 1, p. 29.

[44]Nicola Matteucci, *Lo Stato moderno* (Bologna: Il Mulino,
1997), pp. 135–36.

[45]Edward Coke, *Institutes of the Laws of England*, vol. 1 (London: Society of Stationers, 1628), lib. 2, fol. 97b, sect. 138. The
complete passage from Edward Coke is as follows:

> And this is another strong argument in law, *nihil quod
> est contra rationem est licitum*, for reason is the life

In a customary constitution, reason is immanent, but not the abstract reason of the rationalists; it is rather historical reason in which, in the English legal and political tradition, there is less of a rigid contrast between nature and history. In Matteucci's opinion, even John Locke's great work on natural law essentially speaks of a tradition that became rationalized and universal. Once again, we find the idea that what is natural is that which has evolved.

However, the question of the relationship between Hayek and natural law is certainly not easy to define. For example, Charles Covell came to place Hayek among the "defenders" of natural law, although he makes it clear that he considers Hayek a defender of natural law by virtue of his opposition to legal positivism, rather than for any connection with the natural-law tradition, which is totally lacking in Hayek's work.[46] Covell says that there is another perspective from which Hayek refers to a "natural" model, a perspective that is, in a certain sense, linked to Matteucci's ideas. Covell writes, "Hayek constructed an essentially naturalistic model of law which looked back to the tradition in legal philosophy of Coke and Blackstone."[47] In this way, Hayek rejects both legal positivism, for its constructivism, and also the idea of the

---

of the law nay the common law itself its nothing else but reason; which is to be understood of an artificiall perfection of reason, gotten by long study, observation, and experience. . . . This legal reason est summa ratio. And therefore if all the reason, that is dispersed into so many several heads, were united into one, yet could he not make such a law as the law of England is; because by many successions of ages it hath been fined and refined by an infinite number of grave and learned men, . . . and by long experience growne to a such perfection.

[46]Charles Covell, *The Defence of Natural Law: A Study in the Ideas of Justice in the Writings of Lon L. Fuller, Michael Oakeshott, F.A. Hayek, Ronald Dworkin, and John Finnis* (London: Macmillan, 1992), p. xiii.

[47]Ibid., p. xiv.

rule of law based on a voluntarist model derived from Thomas Hobbes. William Blackstone makes a particular use of the concept of natural law when, in order to demonstrate the moral basis of the English legal system, he defines English law as being based on the principles of natural law, established by God, that the human mind is able to discover. As a result, "the common law had been developed—or rather discovered—by the English courts in accordance with procedures of adjudication in which legal rules and precedents were established through an application to individual cases of the principles of morality and reasonableness that ran through the whole structure of English law."[48]

Thus, we find a "reasonableness" not unlike Edward Coke's reason, which is founded in the common law by virtue of the historical process through which it has developed. Hayek favors English common law, law *discovered* by the judges, creating a spontaneous order. On the contrary, he is against the idea that had taken root in absolutist states, that the act of *making* and *breaking* laws is the essence of sovereignty—a deliberate act of the sovereign's will.

Hayek also takes issue with Cartesian-based rationalism. This school of thought ignores the distinction between *taxis* and *cosmos*, i.e., between systems and associations whose formal structure is characterized by a constructed order, and those systems that, on the contrary, developed and took root by means of an evolutionary process and which could therefore be defined as spontaneous orders. Constructivist rationalism concentrates its attention exclusively on the institutions of the first type, overlooking the fact that intentionally constructed forms of human association are often supported on the wider base of a spontaneous order. Hayek counts the common-law legal system among those that can be characterized as a *cosmos* and ascribes it to the evolutionary rationalism that led to the configuration of the natural process that Covell defines as "legal naturalism."[49] Covell explains that, in

---

[48]Ibid., p. 3.

[49]Ibid., p. 143.

this sense, for Hayek, "law and legal institutions should be examined in their relation to the processes which governed the evolution of the customary and tradition-based practices embedded in actual historical communities."[50] Having said this, it should nevertheless be emphasized that Hayek is above all a great defender of the rule of law and that he prefers the concept of cultural evolution to that of human nature.

The truly irreconcilable points between the evolutionist theory of law and Rothbard's adherence to the concept of natural law are rationalism and fallibilism. One of Rothbard's severest reprimands is, in fact, "Hayek's continuous and all-pervasive attack on reason."[51] In reality, Hayek's attack is against the abuse of reason, against that constructive rationalism that leads to an infinite faith in the capacity of human reason to shape social and political institutions as it pleases. In order to avoid any misunderstandings, it should be noted that Hayek is not an anti-rationalist, saying, "it is therefore better in this connection not to distinguish between 'rationalism' and 'anti-rationalism' but to distinguish between a constructivist and an evolutionary, or, in Karl Popper's terms, a naïve and a critical rationalism."[52]

Given these premises, Rothbard is unable to share the Hayekian idea of true and false individualism, which contrasts a rationalist tradition that is mainly French (in the Cartesian mold and moving toward a constructivist presumption) with a British, evolutionist, empirical and truly liberal tradition connected by Hayek to the Whig tradition. Rothbard criticizes the fact that thinkers of the caliber of Thomas Jefferson, Richard Price, Joseph Priestley, and Thomas Paine were undervalued and seen as "terrible rationalists." Rothbard makes a further comment, and one that

---

[50]Ibid., p. 128.

[51]Rothbard, "Memo to the Volker Fund on F.A. Hayek's *Constitution of Liberty*"; see p. 61 in this volume.

[52]Hayek, *Law, Legislation, and Liberty*, vol. 1, p. 29.

seems justified, concerning Hayek's having overlooked the French liberal thinkers of the nineteenth century—such as Frédéric Bastiat, Gustave de Molinari, and Charles Dunoyer.[53] (Molinari, of course, was Belgian but was closely associated with the French liberals.) Ralph Raico recently made a similar criticism of the Hayekian categories of true and false individualism, among other things highlighting the fact that there is a great liberal tradition in France, represented by Benjamin Constant, Alexis de Tocqueville, and Jean-Baptiste Say, besides the abovementioned Bastiat, Molinari, and Dunoyer.[54]

Thus, faith in the rational capacities of man to discover and correctly interpret the laws of nature and absolute ethical values is not really compatible with the evolutionist and fallibilist position. The foundations of liberty are completely different for Hayek and Rothbard. Hayek bases the reasons for liberty on our ignorance. The necessary starting point for his theory of a liberal society is fallibility, partiality, and the

---

[53]Rothbard, "Memo to the Volker Fund on F.A. Hayek's *Constitution of Liberty*"; see p. 61 in this volume.

[54]Ralph Raico, "La tradizione liberale francese dell'Ottocento," *Federalismo e libertà* 5–6 (settembre-dicembre 2001), pp. 171–207. According to Raico, the Hayekian distinction actually introduces a fair amount of confusion. Raico notes that, among other things, Molinari proposed a conception of the evolution of society that was very close to Hayek's (p. 191). Raico thinks that it is Bastiat's and Molinari's tradition that had a decisive influence on the Italian liberals after the mid-nineteenth century and, through them, on the Public Choice School of thought. It is, however, worth recalling what Hayek writes about Tocqueville in "Individualism: True and False":

> In the nineteenth century I find it represented most perfectly in the work of two of its greatest historians and political philosophers, Alexis de Tocqueville and Lord Acton. These two men seem to me to have more successfully developed what was best in the political philosophy of the Scottish philosophers, Burke, and the English Whigs than any other writers I know.

See F.A. Hayek, *Individualism and Economic Order* (Chicago: University of Chicago Press), p. 4.

scattering of knowledge among particular situations in time and place among millions and millions of people. Given this, liberty becomes a direct consequence of the sharing and spreading of knowledge, which is a necessary condition for the unique and limited knowledge of individuals to be used in the best way. A liberal society in which there is peaceful cooperation and the division of labor is one that "can make use of so much more knowledge than the mind of the wisest ruler could comprehend."[55] The value of individual liberty

> rests chiefly on the recognition of the inevitable ignorance of all of us concerning a great many of the factors on which the achievement of our ends and welfare depends. If there were omniscient men, if we could know not only all that affects the attainment of our present wishes but also our future wants and desires, there would be little case for liberty. . . . Liberty is essential in order to leave room for the unforeseeable and unpredictable; we want it because we have learned to expect from it the opportunity of realizing many of our aims.[56]

For Rothbard, on the other hand, human ignorance is too uncertain a basis for liberty.[57] According to the *authentic rationalist theory*, we should be able to know what is best for man and to found absolute values on human nature.[58] Rothbard dismisses the Hayekian premises as an "attack on man's reason."[59] It seems to me, however, that precisely on

---

[55]F.A. Hayek, *The Constitution of Liberty* (Chicago: University of Chicago Press, 1960), p. 31.

[56]Ibid., p. 29.

[57]Rothbard, "Letter on *The Constitution of Liberty* by F.A. Hayek"; see p. 71 in this volume.

[58]Rothbard, "Memo to the Volker Fund on F.A. Hayek's *Constitution of Liberty*"; see p. 61 in this volume.

[59]Ibid.

this point, Rothbard's position is even more debatable. The proposed anchoring of absolute values on a hypothetical eternal and unchanging kind of human nature raises legitimate questions. Norberto Bobbio, a supporter of the historicity of rights, contests the possibility of effectively searching for an absolute foundation when he says,

> For centuries this illusion was common among advocates of the natural law, who believed they had safeguarded certain rights from any possible confutation by deducing them from human nature (although the rights were not always the same). However, human nature has proved to be a very shaky foundation on which to build an absolute principle for incontrovertible rights. . . . Human rights constitute a variable category as is adequately demonstrated by the history of the last few centuries. The list of human rights has been modified and continues to be modified in changing historical circumstances: the requirements and interests of the ruling classes, the available means for their enactment, technological developments, etc. . . . Thus rights are not fundamental by their nature. That which appears to be fundamental in a given historical era or civilization, is not fundamental in other eras or civilizations.[60]

Guido Fassò emphasizes the role played by the doctrine of natural law as a means of rationalizing the law and as a basis for constitutionalism, but he adds that in order to preserve its function as a bulwark of liberty, natural law "must stop trying to express a system of absolute values, given for all time, outside history."[61] This is an invitation to recover an

---

[60]Norberto Bobbio, *The Age of Rights*, trans. Allen Cameron (Cambridge: Blackwell, 1996), pp. 4–6.

[61]Fassò, *La legge della ragione*, p. 217. (All translations are my own unless otherwise noted.) Dario Antiseri, regarding the possibility of establishing absolute values, poses the following questions:

awareness of the historical and evolutionary character of law. Fassò goes on to say that it would be ingenuous "to mistake the values held in one age, and valid for that age, for eternal and immutable values."[62]

Thus, the attempt to establish what is absolutely good for man by appealing to "human nature," which would really seem to be a cultural idea, demonstrates the great distance between Rothbard and Hayek's evolutionary argument. In this sense, Rothbard's criticism of Hayek is paradigmatic of the split we find today within the Austrian School of economics between the libertarians who refer back to Locke's version of the idea of right reason that enables an understanding of natural law, and the heirs of the theory, typical of the Austrian School, of a limited, fallible, and evolutionist kind of knowledge. This contrast, already evident in the writings under consideration here, is made explicit and theorized more fully by Rothbard in his 1992 *The Present State of the Austrian School of Economics*, from which the profound differences between the various paradigms within the Austrian School emerge. In this paper, Rothbard takes his distance from "Hayek's entire work," in that it is "devoted to a denigration of human reason."[63]

> Absolute values for whom? Absolute on the basis of which arguments? Absolute because they are experienced as such or because they are based on absolute reasons? . . . And is it not true that nothing is more cultural than the idea of *nature* and, therefore, also of human *nature*? And then, is it not precisely the awareness of the fallibility of human knowledge and of an inevitable pluralism of different values that provides the safest garrison for liberty and the constitutional state?

See Antiseri, "Ius quia iustum. Sed quid iustum? Considerazioni in margine a 'La dottrina del diritto naturale'," in *Alessandro Passerin d'Entrèves pensatore europeo*, p. 111.

[62]Fassò, La legge della ragione, p. 217

[63]Murray N. Rothbard, in *The Logic of Action I*, p. 141. This work was first presented on the occasion of the Tenth Anniversary

Rothbard rightly points out that not all that has evolved spontaneously is consistent with a system of liberty and an open society. It would therefore be a mistake to accept passively all conventions and customs for the simple reason that they have already been established. According to the idea of cultural evolution, over the passage of time, the customs and institutions that take root are those best suited to the survival and development of a social group. Thus, if the Rothbardian criticism of Hayek as a historian of political thought does not seem to grasp the essence of his reflections, Rothbard does, however, highlight one of the more problematic areas of Hayek's work. It is not only questionable whether the best institutions are always the ones to succeed, but there is also the problem of the long period of time required for the necessary changes to take place in any unfair institutions or customs. As a matter of fact, Hayek does not rule out the possibility of deliberate legislative corrections:

Austrian Scholar's Conference. In it, Rothbard highlights the differences within the Austrian School of economics regarding the dichotomy between the Hayekian paradigm and that of Mises on the subject of unintended consequences which would, in effect, undermine the importance of the intended consequences of an individual's rational plans. If, as Mises maintains, all human actions have a purpose, in Rothbard's opinion it would be much better to make intentional and known all that which is at the unintentional level. Rothbard criticizes the Hayekian theory of spontaneous order since, from his point of view, it implies a lack of awareness on the part of human beings. Besides, accepting such a theory would mean holding a conservative and uncritical attitude towards those institutions that had simply developed spontaneously, the state included. It is necessary, however, to emphasize that in this paper Rothbard does not address the subject of the criticism of the value-free defense of the market sustained by Mises. In order to understand the divisions between the Austrians, it is instructive to read the article by Joseph T. Salerno, "Ludwig von Mises as Social Rationalist," *Review of Austrian Economics* 4, no. 1 (1990): 26–54. Salerno contrasts Mises's "rationalism" with Hayek's "irrational" emphasis on spontaneous order. Salerno's idea is that to achieve social change, we cannot rely on spontaneous and unintended consequences (pp. 50–51).

> The fact that all law arising out of the necessity to articulate rules of conduct will of necessity possess some desirable properties not necessarily possessed by the commands of a legislator does not mean that in other respects such law may not develop in very undesirable directions, and that when this happens correction by deliberate legislation may not be the only practicable way out. For a variety of reasons the spontaneous process of growth may lead into an impasse from which it cannot extricate itself by its own forces or which it will at least not correct quickly enough. . . . But such occasions when it is recognized that some hereto accepted rules are unjust in the light of more general principles of justice may well require the revision not only of single rules but whole sections of the established system of case law.[64]

Therefore, even if reason does not have a planning and creative role in the field of the establishment of institutions, it is able and indeed *has* to play a corrective role. Covell underlines the fact that Hayek is not really barrenly anchored to tradition; rather he recognizes the fact that, "a system of predominantly judge-made law—such as English law—always stood in need of correction and amendment through an institutional procedure of statutory legislation."[65]

Moreover, it is perhaps worth noting that the concept of evolution is not completely foreign to Rothbardian ideas, even if it is not one of his characteristic lines of thought. In *For a New Liberty*, Rothbard makes reference to the development of the common law when he considers the possibility of a libertarian legal code. In doing so, Rothbard uses the same theoretical instruments as Bruno Leoni, who, as Raimondo Cubeddu notes, assimilates the rule of law to "the

---

[64]Hayek, *Law, Legislation, and Liberty*, vol. 1, pp. 88–89

[65]Covell, *The Defense of Natural Law*, p. 132.

very same process of spontaneous social evolution that includes the market, religion, law and language."[66]

On this basis, Rothbard thinks that Hayek is a conservative, even if Hayek denies this in his concluding essay in *The Constitution of Liberty*, "Why I Am Not a Conservative." Explaining the reasons he rejects conservatism, Hayek writes,

> the main point about liberalism is that it wants to go elsewhere, not to stand still. . . . It has never been a backward-looking doctrine. . . . Liberalism is not averse to evolution and change; and where spontaneous change has been smothered by government control, it wants a great deal of change of policy. . . . It would seem to the liberal, indeed, that what is most urgently needed in most parts of the world is a thorough sweeping away of the obstacles to free growth . . . the admiration of the conservatives for free growth generally applies only to the past . . . one of the fundamental traits of the conservative attitude is a fear of change, a timid distrust of the new as such. . . . It is, indeed, part of the liberal attitude to assume that, especially in the economic field, the self-regulating forces of the market will somehow bring about the required adjustments to new conditions, although no one can foretell how they will do this in a particular instance.[67]

Besides, Hayek's attitude toward American institutions makes clear his position regarding tradition; he explains that "to the liberal they are valuable not mainly because they are long established or because they are American but because they correspond to the ideals which he cherishes."[68] Thus,

---

[66]Raimondo Cubeddu, Introduction to *La libertà e la legge*, by Bruno Leoni (Macerata, Italy: Liberilibri, 1994), p. xiii.

[67]Hayek, *The Constitution of Liberty*, pp. 399–400.

[68]Ibid., p. 399.

Hayek denies being a conservative, since he believes in free competition and in change. As observed by Sergio Ricossa in his introduction to the Italian edition of *The Constitution of Liberty*, "when you are for life, free growth, and spontaneous evolution, it is not possible to have greater esteem for a conservative party in the strict sense than a driver has for the brakes of his car, even if they are extremely useful."[69]

The authors of the introduction to the Italian edition of *Law, Legislation, and Liberty* find the demarcation line between conservatism and Hayekian thought in the fact that the great value of tradition lies, for Hayek, in its rational nature, because it has developed by means of an evolutionary and competitive process. In this way, the value of tradition does not consist in the "mere fact of there being traditions," a characteristic feature of authentic conservative and reactionary thought.[70]

CRITICISM OF THE
CONCEPT OF COERCION IN HAYEK

THE CONCEPT OF COERCION is one of the issues that arouses Rothbard's polemic force. He in part approves of Hayek's initial definition of liberty as an "absence of interpersonal coercion," but he considers that it marks the beginning of

---

[69]Sergio Ricossa, Introduction to *La società libera*, by F.A. Hayek, trans. Marcella Bianchi di Lavagna Malagodi (Florence, Italy: Vallecchi Editore, 1969), p. 10.

[70]A.M. Petroni and S. Monti Bragadin, Introduction to *F.A. Hayek, Legge, legislazione e libertà*, trans. Pier Giuseppe Monateri (Milano, Italy: Il Saggiatore, 1989), p. xxii.

Hayek's "descent into the abyss."[71] For Rothbard, the idea of coercion as a threat or intent to harm is excessively broad since it would allow, the possibility of identifying both a variety of coercive situations requiring protection by the government, but also a whole range of government activities that are not really coercive.

Here, it is first of all necessary to clear up a misunderstanding. As Hayek was keen to emphasize, the most significant thing in *The Constitution of Liberty* is not so much the definition of liberty as an absence of coercion, but rather as "that condition of men in which coercion of some by others is reduced as much as is possible in society."[72] Rothbard felt that coercion was the use of "physical violence or the threat thereof."[73] According to Hayek, "By 'coercion' we mean such control of the environment or circumstances of a person by another that, in order to avoid greater evil, he is forced to act not according to a coherent plan of his own, but to serve the ends of another." He goes on to say that, "Coercion

---

[71]Rothbard, "Memo to the Volker Fund on F.A. Hayek's *Constitution of Liberty*"; see p. 61 in this volume.

[72]Hayek, *Constitution of Liberty*, p. 11; F.A. Hayek, *Studies in Philosophy, Politics and Economics* (London: Routledge and Kegan Paul, 1967), p. 348. Here Hayek replies to the criticisms made by Ronald Hamowy in a 1961 review. Cf. Ronald Hamowy, "Hayek's Concept of Freedom: A Critique," *New Individualist Review* 1, no. 1 (1961): 28–31. Hamowy's reasoning was very close to that of Rothbard. Hayek's many concessions to the role of government led to numerous criticisms on the part of libertarian thinkers. See Ronald Hamowy, "Freedom and the Rule of Law in F.A. Hayek," *Il politico* (1971–1972): 355–56; "Law and the Liberal Society: F.A. Hayek's Constitution of Liberty," *Journal of Libertarian Studies* 2, no. 4 (1978): 287–97; John N. Gray, "F.A. Hayek on Liberty and Tradition," *Journal of Libertarian Studies* 4, no. 2 (1980): 119–37. Rothbard's criticism of the Hayekian concept of coercion can be found in "Hayek on Coercion and Freedom," *Literature of Liberty* (Winter 1980): 53–54. See also *Ethics of Liberty*, pp. 219–29.

[73]Rothbard, "Memo to the Volker Fund on F.A. Hayek's *Constitution of Liberty*"; see p. 61 in this volume.

occurs when one man's actions are made to serve another man's will, not for his own but for the other's purpose."[74]

Hayek gave some examples to show clear cases of coercion; for example, the case of dismissal or threat of dismissal in periods of widespread unemployment, or in a mining town where the only possible work is as a miner. However, in Rothbard's opinion, these cases do not demonstrate coercion, since the mine owner is only exercising his legitimate right of refusing "to make any further exchanges with one or more people."[75] Another example of coercion given by Hayek was the case of the sole owner of a spring in an oasis who forces the local inhabitants to accept arbitrary conditions in order to obtain any water. Yet another possible case is that of the only doctor available who, in the face of a serious epidemic, refuses to treat any patients or requests exorbitant fees. In these cases, Rothbard thought that the subjects in question were simply exercising their own rights of private property or their rights to choose whether to engage in professional relations or not. Hayek nevertheless maintains that these are cases in which coercive government action would be justified in order to avoid a worse kind of coercion. He considers that some goods and services are essential for survival and therefore, "It is because these services are regarded as rights to be counted upon that a refusal to render them except on unusual terms is justly regarded as a harmful alteration of the environment and therefore as coercion."[76]

Hayek's point is that in any case coercion

> cannot be altogether avoided, because the only way to prevent it is by the threat of coercion. Free society has met this problem by conferring the monopoly of coercion on the state and by attempting to

---

[74]Hayek, *Constitution of Liberty*, pp. 20–21, 133.

[75]Rothbard, *The Ethics of Liberty*, p. 220.

[76]Hayek, *Studies in Philosophy, Politics and Economics*, p. 350.

limit this power of the state to instances where it is required to prevent coercion by private persons. This is possible only by the state's protecting known private spheres of the individuals against interference by others and delimiting these private spheres, not by specific assignation, but by creating conditions under which the individual can determine his own sphere by relying on rules which tell him what the government will do in different types of situations.[77]

For Rothbard, however, the point is not to try to reduce coercion to a minimum by means of acts of coercion, but rather to eliminate it entirely, in that it is unjust and immoral. Rothbard's position is usually of an *integral* kind, one that brooks no compromise. Obviously, he rejects the idea that a free society could grant the state a monopoly on coercion and that it could thus defend individuals from coercion, since, in his opinion, the state is itself the principal aggressor in society:

> Therefore, since liberty requires the elimination of aggressive violence in society . . . the State is not, and can never be, justified as a defender of liberty. For the State lives by its very existence on the two-fold and pervasive employment of aggressive violence against the very liberty and property of individuals that it is supposed to be defending.[78]

In Rothbard's second comment on *Constitution of Liberty*, he gives a long list of state activities that Hayek considers justified and that he himself rejects categorically. These are functions ranging from public health to state provision of roads, state aid for the poor, government subsidies in the public interest, obligatory old-age pensions, and also include

---

[77]Hayek, *Constitution of Liberty*, p. 21.

[78]Rothbard, *The Ethics of Liberty*, p. 224.

conscription in the event of foreign aggression, and many other typical government activities. Conscription, for example, is one of those issues about which libertarians are totally intransigent, considering it a form of downright slavery.

Hayek, instead, thinks it is certainly a very severe form of coercion but one that could be justified "to ward off the danger of worse coercion by an external enemy."[79] The question of public health and of various kinds of welfare for the poor is part of the particular Hayekian concept of solidarity. Hayek feels that it goes without saying that the state should take care of those unable to provide for themselves and that a minimum level of subsistence should be guaranteed for all so that no member of society would lack for food, shelter, and medical treatment. Apart from proven cases of need that should rightly be borne by society as a whole, in reality Hayek proposes solutions to social-security problems that are not based on a state monopoly for certain activities. He only opts for obligatory insurance in fields such as old-age pensions and health care, on the basis of the observation that if certain state activities enjoy a monopoly, "the result is usually not only that those advantages soon prove illusory but that the character of the services becomes entirely different from that which they would have had if provided by competing agencies."[80] In this way, the benefits of competition are lost and certain services become the dominion of bureaucratic hierarchies. For Hayek, it is precisely in order to safeguard some individuals from suffering coercion that state activities cannot be limited to maintaining law and order. Obligatory insurance, which Rothbard sees as invading the sphere of an individual's liberty, means that the other members of society are not obliged to provide for other members in need.

The Hayekian argument concerning solidarity is linked to a particular conception. In a society in which the protective

---

[79]Hayek, *Studies in Philosophy, Politics and Economics*, p. 349.

[80]Hayek, *Constitution of Liberty*, p. 261.

institutions of traditional society are no longer able to provide a safety net, it is only right that the community should assume the burden of the most critical situations. The legitimate functions of the state cannot be limited to ensuring observance of the law and defending the country against external enemies.

> There is, however, yet another class of common risks with regard to which the need for government has until recently not been generally admitted and where as the result of the dissolution of the ties of the local community, and of the development of a highly mobile open society, an increasing number of people are no longer closely associated with particular groups whose help and support they can count upon in the case of misfortune. The problem here is chiefly the fate of those who for various reasons cannot make their living in the market, such as the sick, the old, the physically or mentally defective, the widows and orphans—that is all people suffering from adverse conditions which may affect anyone and against which most individuals cannot alone make adequate provision but in which a society that has reached a certain level of wealth can afford to provide for all.
>
> The assurance of a certain minimum income for everyone, or a sort of floor below which nobody need fall even when he is unable to provide for himself, appears not only to be wholly legitimate protection against a risk common to all, but a necessary part of the Great Society in which the individual no longer has specific claims on the members of the particular small group into which he was born.[81]

---

[81]F.A. Hayek, *Law, Legislation, and Liberty,* vol. 3, *The Political Order of a Free People* (Chicago: University of Chicago Press, 1979), pp. 54–55.

Hayek justifies the fact that the state raises funds through taxation in order to offer a whole range of services that, for various reasons, cannot be supplied by the market. Regarding, for example, the management of public leisure services, theaters, public parks, or goods of cultural value, he favors decentralized management, not control at the national level. Alternatively, management could be entrusted to private institutions that would act as intermediaries, albeit he has no objections in principle to the public management of these goods.[82]

A particularly sensitive point on which Hayek manages to provoke Rothbard's criticism is education. Hayek is obviously not in favor of a state monopoly on education, since he is well aware of the dangers inherent in uniformity. He is for the widest possible pluralism and for competition in the field of education. He writes, "Indeed, the very possibility that, with a system of government education, all elementary education may come to be dominated by the theories of a particular group . . . should be sufficient to warn us of the risks involved in subjecting the whole educational system to central direction."[83] Nevertheless, not only is he in favor of compulsory school attendance, but he also approves of the school-voucher system proposed by Milton Friedman. So, while he rules out a state educational system, he accepts the idea of public funding for schools. He says that

> this does not mean, however, that compulsory education or even government-financed general education today requires the educational institutions to be run by the government. . . . As has been shown by Professor Milton Friedman, it would now be entirely practicable to defray the costs of general education out of the public purse

---

[82]For the management of natural parks and the cultural heritage, Hayek gives the example of the famous and very efficient English National Trust.

[83]Hayek, *Constitution of Liberty*, p. 380.

without maintaining government schools, by giving the parents vouchers covering the costs of education for each child which they could hand over to schools of their choice. It may still be desirable that government directly provide schools in a few isolated communities where the number of children is too small. . . . But with respect to the great majority of the population, it would undoubtedly be possible to leave the organization and management of education entirely to private efforts, with the government providing merely the basic finance and ensuring a minimum standard for all schools where the vouchers could be spent.[84]

These ideas are included on Rothbard's list of Hayek's partisan biases at the end of Rothbard's review, "Letter on *The Constitution of Liberty* by F.A. von Hayek." For this anarcho-capitalist, these are positions he cannot share, since, in his opinion, any public funding—and indeed anything pertaining to the state—should simply cease to exist.

Thus, for Rothbard, Hayek has not reached the target of establishing and defending liberty. The principle of the rule of law is itself too vague a concept and in any case insufficient as a principle on which to base the defense of liberty. For Hayek, the rule of law is the principal instrument with which to defend individual liberty. He explains that, "the rule of law constitutes a limitation on the powers of all government, including the powers of the legislature."[85] For the rule of law to prevail in a society, each law must meet certain basic requirements: it has to be general and abstract, known and certain and, lastly, it has to be the same for all. The function of the rule of law is to create the conditions within which individuals can act freely and follow their own goals on the basis of their own knowledge. Hayek feels that, "the task of the lawgiver is not to set up a particular order

[84]Ibid., pp. 378, 381.

[85]Ibid., p. 205.

but merely to create conditions in which an orderly arrangement can establish and ever renew itself."[86]

Hayek's response to Ronald Hamowy's criticisms provides a useful explanation of the function of the rule of law:

> It is the distinguishing mark of the Western political tradition that . . . coercion has been confined to instances where it is required by general abstract rules, known beforehand and equally applicable to all . . . combined with the requirement that such general rules authorizing coercion could be justified only by the general purpose of preventing worse coercion . . . this principle seems to be as effective a method of minimizing coercion as mankind has yet discovered. It seems to me the best protection yet devised against that administrative despotism which is the greatest danger to individual liberty today.[87]

Roberta A. Modugno

---

[86]Ibid., p. 161.

[87]Hayek, *Studies in Philosophy, Politics and Economics*, p. 350. Hayek responds to Hamowy's article mentioned above, "Hayek's Concept of Freedom: A Critique."

Reviews and Comments by
Murray Newton Rothbard

1.

LETTER ON
"RUGGED INDIVIDUALISM" BY GEORGE B. CUTTEN

November 16, 1948
Dr. F.A. Harper
Foundation for Economic Education

Dear Dr. Harper:

I apologize for the delay in commenting on Dr. Cutten's speech expounding rugged individualism.[1] As a matter of fact, I was just going to write you a letter on election night, and tuned in the radio expecting to hear the returns confirming the expected results in a "dull" election. I need not explain how my attention was diverted.

Since then, I have been recuperating from and analyzing the results. My forecast on the political history of the USA in the next few years is briefly this: Truman and Congress will believe that they now have a mandate for running headlong down a steep shortcut on the old Road to Serfdom.[2] They will show no hesitation in acting accordingly. The Republicans will

---

[1]G.B. Cutten, "Rugged Individualism," in *Vital Speeches of the Day* (November 5, 1934). This was a paper given by George Burton Cutten, president of Colgate University on the occasion of a university meeting, September 20, 1934.

[2]The "Road to Serfdom" refers to the work by F.A. Hayek, *The Road to Serfdom* (Chicago: Chicago University Press, 1944).

promptly "reorganize," "meaning simply that the recent (and forthcoming) accretions of State power are here to stay . . . and that . . . they are preparing to dispose themselves most advantageously in a contest for their control and management."[3]

In 1952, we shall be treated to a "contest" between a Douglas-Bowles or Humphrey-Bowles ticket versus a Stassen-Saltonstall ticket, if indeed Stassen is not considered by that time as an "ultrareactionary."[4] The New Deal-ish voters will all vote for Douglas-Bowles while the substantial minority of true liberal voters will "go fishing" in disgust. The consequence will be a thumping Democratic landslide and four more years of even more socialism.

In 1956 . . . well who knows whether elections themselves may not be "outmoded" by that time?

As for Dr. Cutten's speech, I found it very interesting, particularly since it is the first document I've received from the foundation with which I find myself in almost complete disagreement.

The philosophy of *rugged individualism* has always seemed to me to be not only a useless but also a pernicious outgrowth or variant of *individualism*. Rugged individualism, also known as social Darwinism, is inhumane and illogical; it is based on a completely false use of analogy and an absurd theory of ethics.

The theory is originally based on an unwarranted extension of Darwinism to the history of man. Supposedly, man develops continually struggling against nature—i.e., struggling to

---

[3]Rothard notes, A.J. Nock, *Our Enemy, the State* (New York: William Morrow, 1935), p. 20.

[4]Paul Douglas (1892–1976) was a U.S. senator (Democrat); Chester Bowles (1901–1986) was a U.S. congressman (Democrat) and diplomat; Hubert Humphrey (1911–1978) was vice president of the United States from 1965 to 1969; Harold Stassen (1907–2001) was a U.S. senator (Republican). In 1948 and many times thereafter, Stassen ran for the Republican presidential nomination, but he was always defeated; Leverett Saltonstall was a U.S. senator (Republican).

adapt himself to natural conditions. As generations develop, the "fit" or "the fittest" survive, and the "unfit" die. The progeny of the "fit" are also "fit," while the unfit get no chance to reproduce. In this way the human race supposedly improves. As Dr. Cutten puts it, "The strong won, the weak lost; the strong left progeny, the weak died early and child-less. It worked out pretty well too."[5]

The theory waxes ever more lyrical about the beauty and wisdom of this process of "natural selection." Ah, all-wise, all-knowing, and benevolent Nature! All Nature's energies work toward the improvement of the human race. Does Nature seem to be unkind and cruel and opposed to the Christian ethic? Nonsense! That is because Nature is truly benevolent and far sighted; man's attempts to be kind are merely examples of his shortsightedness. Hands off! Let Nature do the job, "the cleaning and selecting process."

Let Dr. Cutten continue the panegyric:

> For . . . over a million years . . . old mother nature has been experimenting, and has come to the undoubted conclusion that rugged individualism is the most successful brand of biped and that the rugged individualist is worth saving. She is very careful of those who lift and very careless of those who lean. When nature has decided that an indi-vidual is a confirmed leaner, she hurries to get rid of him forthwith lest he should contaminate the race which she is so carefully trying to develop.[6]

How did this careful and farseeing selection take place? Dr. Cutten becomes specific:

> Man's extremity was nature's opportunity for then came the time of most severe competition. Glacial periods, famine floods, and other similar calamities

---

[5]Cutten, "Rugged Individualism," p. 70.

[6]Ibid.

were the days of eliminating the unfit . . . crude . . .
but effective.[7]

After hypnotizing himself into believing that he can gaze
into a crystal ball and divine exactly what Nature is doing, who
she is, and what her motives are, the Rugged Individualist
then returns to the cave, as in Plato, to advise us poor mor-
tals who have not as yet "seen the light." Horrors! He finds
that men are violating Nature's wishes and injunctions, that
the unfit are being protected by "modern medicine and modern philanthropy"[8] and are debilitating the race by being permitted to live and have children. The Rugged Individualist
reluctantly admits that he will never be able to convince us
weaklings to abandon penicillin, hospitals, and soft arm-
chairs. So, he very generously compromises and comes up
with this magnificent solution: "the broadest application of
sterilization." In other words, the unfit will be magnanimously
permitted to live, but not to pollute the racial stream." Thus
will our "responsibility for posterity" be fulfilled.[9]

That is the essence of Dr. Cutten's thesis and the broad
outlines of social Darwinism or rugged individualism. It
seems to me that the mere statement of it would expose it
as obvious bilge. Apparently not, however, since this philosophy had a considerable vogue, and Dr. Cutten apparently
believes in it wholeheartedly. Demolition is therefore in
order, although there are so many fallacies it will be difficult
to treat them more than sketchily.

1. The Absurd Mysticism about Nature

First, I see no validity whatever in this making nature an
anthropomorphic figure Nature. This mystic absurdity
Nature apparently is cast in the image of man, with human
feelings, desires, and attributes. She is strong, farseeing,

---

[7]Ibid., p. 71.

[8]Ibid., p. 70.

[9]Ibid.

and truly kind, etc. All this may be permissible in theology, where apparently anything goes, but not in political philosophy where we are supposedly dealing with the world of facts and not a world of dreams. Nature is simply the environment on earth in which man finds himself, and to treat it as a separate being in the image of man is sheer nonsense.

Second, the Rugged Individualist not only blandly asserts the existence of such a being, but also claims that he has an exclusive pipeline on her wishes, desires, etc. Who is he to speak for Nature? I could with equal validity propound the doctrine that "Nature" is an evil old hag who is trying her best to eliminate the human race—all of it. Not only would such a proposition be equally valid with that of the Rugged Individualist, it would probably be more consonant with the facts. And from this proposition an entirely different set of policies would follow.

Third, the *teleological fallacy*. This is the doctrine that all of the history of man has some sort of deep purpose and goal ordained divinely or by "Nature." This conceives of history with absurd optimism as marching steadily or in zigzag fashion (the Marxists, for example, believe in the zigzag path) toward some "good" goal, which usually by some strange coincidence turns out to be the very goal that the one who propounds the theory desires! Thus, the Marxist sees history as a grand march toward the socialist society of his dreams, and the Rugged Individualist sees history as a grand march of weeding out the "unfit" and improving the race. In both cases there is a grand design and in both cases the design is one that suits the man who propounds it.

Again, this teleology will pass in the confines of the church but not in a discussion of political or social philosophy. In these latter realms it is simply mystic nonsense, with no basis in fact or human experience whatsoever.

2. The Fallacy of the "Survival of the Fittest"

The entire concept of the "fit" surviving is a complete fallacy. Let us suppose that several thousand hard-working, industrious people are working in the fields, while one lazy good-for-nothing is sleeping on a hill. Suddenly, the river-bank near-by gives way and the fields are completely flooded. All the good thrifty people are drowned, while the lazy loafer is the only one who survives. Are we to infer from this that the loafer has been "proved" to be "fit," or has passed some obscure test of "fitness" while the other people have failed the test and are now proved "unfit"? What, then, is the "test"? Where is benevolent Nature now?

And what of the surviving loafer? What is he "fit" for? What superiority has he demonstrated over the others? One and only one "test" has he passed that the others failed, and that is . . . survival. By sheer luck he survived while the others didn't.

Thus, since the loafer's only "fitness" is survival, we see that this alleged process of "survival of the fittest" is a complete and meaningless tautology, simply meaning nothing more nor less than "the survival of those who have survived."

It is therefore evident that there is no moral or ethical value attaching to a survivor. Sheer luck plays the biggest part in history in determining who has survived. The Rugged Individualist suffers from the delusion that survival—sheer survival—is *ipso facto* evidence of high moral qualities. There is no justification for this whatever, as was evident from the above example.

Even take another example, where there is a clear-cut case of the "strong" triumphing over the "weak." Take the case of two hypothetical cavemen, Ug and Ob. Ug is a strong and mighty hunter; he can kill a tiger at a hundred paces, track deer, etc. Ob is not too good at hunting, only good enough to eke out subsistence; he is weak of frame and doesn't like exercise. But Ob likes to paint pictures on the wall, he likes to meditate on life and the world, he likes to write symbols and make sounds on a primitive gourd. Ug is contemptuous, and one day he confiscates Ob's skins and food and kills him. It wasn't much of a fight.

Well, there you are. The "stronger" has won; the "weaker" has lost; but with him was lost the faint precious stirrings of a civilized culture. Where does morality stand on this issue? Has "good" triumphed? Does might make right? Does morality mean barbarism? As far I am concerned, the answer to these questions is a ringing nay!

The Rugged Individualist who gave three lusty cheers on the Ug victory is thus sadly deficient in moral sense. His theory of ethics is on the level of an intolerant barbarian.

3. The Glorification of Struggle

The Rugged Individualist glorifies struggle and condemns the easy path. Since the whole process of civilization has been the cumulative attempt to make it easier to satisfy man's desires, the Rugged Individualist is of necessity opposed to civilization. We consider man as progressing when he invents ever new ways to "reduce costs" which is simply the process of finding easier ways to satisfy man's ever-growing desires.

I consider one of the glories of economic freedom and individualism (not rugged, but humane) the ever-growing standard of living, the magnificent increase in opportunities for leisure, and the development of life-giving modern medicine. I consider it a tribute to the moral qualities of an individualist society that private charity and philanthropy helps the unfortunate people in our midst. Private philanthropy is the direct expression of the great Christian principle of the brotherhood of man and the Golden Rule.

Private philanthropy indeed is the only valid expression of these Christian ethical principles; compulsory charity through "social legislation" is the exact contrary: it is the evil imposition of force by one group on another. Christ was a great individualist not because He was rugged, as Dr. Cutten seems to think, but because He recognized that His great ethical principles could only be put into effect through the voluntary action of individuals and not by a self-appointed group of politician-priests who claim the right to coerce people into adopting the Golden Rule by "social legislation."

The Rugged Individualist, however, disagrees with all this and condemns protection of the "unfit" by minimizing struggle. We all can join in admiring a man who struggles a great deal and finally overcomes all obstacles to achieve a goal. But wouldn't he and everyone be better off if there were fewer obstacles to begin with? Man progresses not by doggedly climbing over obstacles but by eliminating them! This elimination makes the road easier for him and for those who follow. The sum of human happiness is increased. Three cheers certainly for the Pilgrim Fathers who struggled through with no provisions, etc. But wouldn't they have been better off if they had had ample provisions? By glorifying the obstacles, which really are simply impediments to man's happiness, the Rugged Individualist has acquired a peculiarly twisted theory of ethics.

In this sphere there is no final means of scientifically "proving" that the Christian ethic is better than the "rugged" ethic. However, it is clear that Dr. Cutten's dogmatic claim for a scientific basis for the rugged ethic turns out to be simply what I consider to be an absurd theory of ethics.

However, I will say that the Rugged Individualist is entitled to live according to his ethic if he so desires, provided he does not infringe on my right to live according to the Christian ethic. (Dr. Cutten unfortunately does not stay within these limits.) If the statocracy permits individualism to achieve the humane, comfortable, charitable world in the future, I will be content to sit in a cozy armchair watching via television the Rugged Individualist heroically climbing the Matterhorn. Thus, each according to his taste.

4. The Tyranny of the "Scientific" Eugenist

The Rugged Individualist, however, is unfortunately not content to remain within the realm of polite discussion. As with so many other axe grinders, the State is eventually asked to take a hand, and in this case, it plays a very large role indeed. It is "the broadest possible application of sterilization" to prevent "the pollution of the racial stream."[10]

In other words, rugged individualism really turns out to be rugged collectivism. It is difficult to take this monstrous proposal seriously if not for the fact that other people advance it seriously. The example of a successful large-scale carrying out of this principle has been that of one A. Hitler. Do Hitler's experiments seem to be an inhuman, perverse process of extermination? Oh no, the rugged philosopher would say; he simply cleansed the "racial stream."

Of course, Dr. Cutten's "scientific" program of "cleansing" would, I hope, be based on slightly different standards than Hitler's. But what standards? And who is to decide them? Who is going to sterilize whom? Let the State get hold of this mighty instrument and we are going to see the greatest "cleansing" process in history: Negroes, Jews, Asiatics, Catholics, Germans, Russians, Communists, capitalists, Republicans, redheads, people under six feet in height, all people with freckles, non-unionists, etc. Yes, I think that sterilization applied on "the broadest possible" basis can perform a process of "cleansing" that will make the old-fangled glaciers, floods, plagues, and the new-fangled atom bombs and germ warfare look like kindergarten games.

Dr. Cutten may well remonstrate that his sterilizing will be directed by a group of "impartial" expert eugenists. *Quis custodes custodiet?*[11] (Aristotle's great comment on Plato's fascist-eugenist state run by wise, expert guardians: Who will guard the guardians?)

Even if this sterilization were studiously restricted to drunkards, etc., the entire theory is based on the unfounded assumption that the children of the "unfit" are also "unfit"—and similarly for the "fit." Heredity is not that simple. How many sons of mighty kings have turned out to be morons? How many sons of great self-made industrialists

---

[10]Cutten, "Rugged Individualism," p. 70.

[11]This is a shortened version of Juvenal, *Satires VI*, line 347: *Quis custodiet ipsos custodes?*

have turned out to be weaklings? And how many Americans have risen from the ranks of the poor and ignorant? Let us never forget that Beethoven was the son of a confirmed drunkard, a man "unfit" by any eugenic standard. If Dr. Cutten or other "rugged" would-be murderers had been permitted to do their work in that era, the world would have lost a Beethoven. How many unborn geniuses would similarly be slaughtered by the "scientific" rugged eugenists?

When it comes to sterilization, Mr. Rugged Individualist, "kindly include me out." I'm sure my sentiments will be heartily echoed by all the rest of the nonrugged or antirugged individualists. If, Mr. R.I., you grieve because you cannot impart your gift to the world, remember that "charity begins at home."

5. The Fallacy of the "Improvement of the Race"

A fallacy committed by many groups of political philosophers is that somehow an individual living in the present is of far less importance and value than some hypothetical person living in the future.

People of the present are supposed to have a sacred duty to sacrifice themselves on the altar of the "future," for the benefit of some man of the future. Thus, the Marxists justify their unconscionable slaughter as the inevitable birth pangs of a better and happier world of the future.

Aside from the fact that the Marxian-Stalinist future would not be a happy one, I strenuously object to a doctrine that holds a person of the present expendable for the benefit of the future.

The Rugged Individualist, however, justifies slaughter of the present because future individuals are supposedly benefited. "Was nature unkind to the negro when she quietly got rid of the malaria-susceptible members of the race and developed race immunity?"[12] This is merely one example.

---

[12]Cutten, "Rugged Individualism," p. 70.

All this is repugnant to a *true* individualist—to him every individual has equal rights and has equal claim to be treated with justice and to have an opportunity for self-development with freedom.

The "dignity of the individual" means every individual regardless of what era he happens to live in. No one can have the right to sweat the present by any sort of Gosplan—whether Stalinist or rugged—for the benefit of the future, even if the future men actually did benefit, which is of course highly doubtful.

Friedrich Nietzsche, the father of the rugged individualists, said that "Man is a bridge and not a goal—the bridge to the Superman." The humane individualist—the true individualist—says "No! Man himself is the goal; every individual is a goal; no man must be permitted to use any other man as a slave—as a means to any other goal!"

Having presented the reader with this appalling and fallacious doctrine of rugged individualism, Dr. Cutten ends with the usual flourish of desperate alternatives: "Will it be rugged individualism or ragged collectivism? Judge quickly, there is no time to waste."[13]

To a true individualist this is akin to choosing between hanging and the electric chair. However, I feel in the same position as your friend who commented on the choice facing him between liberty and onions or government paternalism and three square meals a day. He chose the latter, albeit reluctantly. Similarly, I would choose ragged collectivism.

It may be that the reason for the general collectivist spirit of modern intellectuals is that they were presented with exactly the same choice by similar people. In other words, the only type of individualism that they came into contact with was the "rugged" type. The inevitable outcome was their choosing ragged collectivism instead, and for that, they are not to be particularly blamed.

---

[13]Ibid., p. 71.

It follows that any widespread distribution of this speech by the foundation would be disastrous to the individualist cause that we all hold so dear. Any converts that may have been made by the uniformly excellent literature that you have distributed until now might very well be lost if people mistakenly believe that all individualism—or that the foundation's individualism—is necessarily rugged.

Granted that there are many statements that have merit in Dr. Cutten's speech; they are more than outweighed by the central thesis. I think that the foundation would do itself a very good turn by (1) not distributing this on a widespread basis, and (2) publishing a critique of "Rugged Individualism" that will completely expose it as really perniciously anti-individualist in spirit and completely fallacious in doctrine.

I'd very much like to know what you, Dr. Harper, think of this problem: should individualism be humane or rugged? Thank you for sending me the speech.

Cordially,

Murray

P.S. I just received Leo Wolman's pamphlet on industry-wide bargaining in the mail. It looks like a fine job. The de Jouvenel pamphlet was also very good, providing an excellent complement to the Stigler and Watts work on rent control.

2.

CONFIDENTIAL MEMO ON F.A. HAYEK'S CONSTITUTION OF LIBERTY

January 21, 1958
To the Volker Fund

F.A. Hayek's *Constitution of Liberty* is, surprisingly and distressingly, an extremely bad, and, I would even say, evil book.[14] Since Hayek is universally regarded, by Right and Left alike, as the leading right-wing intellectual, this will also be an extremely dangerous book. The feeling one gets from reading it is the same sort of feeling I would have gotten if I had been a U.S. senator when Taft got up to support the Wagner public housing bill, or any of his other compromises: i.e., that this tears it.[15] For when the supposed leader of one's movement takes compromising and untenable positions, the opposition can always say: "but even Taft (Hayek)

---

[14]F.A. Hayek, *The Constitution of Liberty* (Chicago: University of Chicago Press, 1960). In this Memorandum, Rothbard refers to the first fourteen chapters of Hayek's manuscript. The Volker Fund had provided a grant for Hayek's work and Rothbard was asked to give his opinion of it.

[15]Robert A. Taft (1889–1953) was a U.S. Senator from 1939 to 1953. Known as "Mr. Republican" for his frontline role in the eponymous party, he was a strong opponent of Roosevelt's New Deal. In 1947 he supported the Taft-Hartley Labor Relations Act. He was against the United States' entry into the Second World War and he further opposed many of the measures adopted during the Cold War period. The Wagner Act (1937) took its name from Senator Robert F. Wagner (Democrat), who was responsible, as a result of the law that bore his name, for the United States Housing Authority, a government agency with the responsibility of providing low-cost housing. In 1949, the question of the right to housing was addressed once again, and the Housing Act was passed—extending the legislation on public housing—with Taft's support.

admits . . ." Hayek is the philosophic counterpart. The only tenable conclusion is that any Volker Fund or any other support for this book will be self-destructive in the highest degree.

In my letter of October 23, 1956, I criticized Hayek's Claremont lectures, which summarized this book, and reference to the letter would be helpful. However, there I wrote that Hayek is a "composite of brilliant things, and very wrong things . . . a mosaic of confusion." In the full-fledged book, the picture and impact change greatly; for the brilliant things fade dismally into the background, and all of Hayek's care and elaboration go into the terribly wrong things. Indeed, this book is a fusion of bad tendencies in his previous books, but which there had been only minor flaws in the product; here the flaws are magnified and raised to the status of a philosophic system. In all the 400 pages, I found only chapters 1 and 10 as agreeable chapters, and all the rest a veritable morass of error and evasion, with almost nothing to relieve the tragedy.

Hayek begins very well by defining freedom as absence of interpersonal coercion and rejecting other definitions. But, in chapter 2, he begins to define *coercion*, and the descent into the abyss begins. For instead of defining coercion as physical violence or the threat thereof, as we would, he defines it to mean *specific acts of one person with the intent of harming another*. He says, for example, that *the reason* why A is firing B, in the free market, is *not* coercion is because A fires him not because he dislikes B, but because keeping him on is uneconomic. The implication is very strong that if A fired B because he hated him, then this would be coercion, and the government *would* have a very strong case for stopping this.

Further, Hayek explicitly states that if a government act is laid down as a general rule in advance, so that the subject can predict its coming, then, *whatever* it is, it is not coercion. He explicitly applies this to the draft: since everyone knows in advance that he will be drafted, it is not coercion! Dr. Harper mentioned this in his comments, but didn't attribute the importance that it has for Hayek. Of course, this also means that if everyone knew in advance that he would be tortured and enslaved one year out of every three, neither would this be coercion. From this ensues Hayek's inordinate passion for the rule of law and equality under the law, which he reveres to the exclusion of all other (and more important) aspects of liberty. If *everyone* were prohibited from drinking or from blaspheming Allah or forced into slavery one out of three years, then Hayek could not say for a moment that this would be coercion or unjustified.

His entire historical section then becomes a mass of distortion, since he interprets the whole libertarian movement as simply a narrow advance toward equality under the law, which is only one, and a minor, aspect of libertarianism. Hayek is enabled to do this by his brusque and cavalier dismissal of the whole theory of natural law (natural rights—the great libertarian deduction from natural law—is not mentioned once in the Hayek discussion) as "intellectually unsatisfying." Since natural law is dismissed as some sort of unimportant quirk, then obviously only the *form* of law can be discussed, rather than the content: i.e., would everybody be equal under whatever law there is? Granted, this restriction of form would, in fact, restrict the content of tyranny to some degree, but Hayek sees only the equality under the law as a value. And not only does he brusquely dismiss natural law and natural rights from his consideration, he acts as if the seventeenth- and eighteenth-century libertarians were not really concerned about it either.

Tied up with his dismissal of natural law is Hayek's continuous and all-pervasive attack on reason. Reason is his *bête noire*, and time and time again, from numerous and even contradictory standpoints, he opposes it. The true rationalist theory was, and is, that reason can discover the natural law of man, and from this can discover the natural rights of liberty. Since Hayek dismisses this even from historical consideration, he is left with only two choices for the formation of a political ethic: *either* blind adherence to custom and the traditions of the "social organism," *or* the coercive force of government edict. The former, to Hayek, is the "evolutionary," irrationalist, empirical (and really, pragmatic) tradition, and is good; the latter is the evil, rationalist, "French" tradition.

In short, for Hayek, reason and rationalism are synonymous with government coercion, and coercion can only be attacked by also attacking reason, and saying, over and over again, that we need to do so, despite the fact that we do not know what we are doing or why. Not realizing that reason is in fact the very *opposite* of coercion, that force and persuasion are antitheses, and that this was so considered by the rationalist libertarians, Hayek constantly confuses traditions and concepts. Also, he doesn't seem to fully realize the paradox of using reason, as he tries to do, to attack reason.

Because he lumps all systematic rationalists together, he can say, with the Jacobins, that reason leads to tyranny, and a few pages later, attack rationalism that leads to "extreme" *laissez-faire*, and even anarchism. He explicitly attacks *laissez-faire* for being the product of "French" rationalism—and he is right that it is such a product—but out of what masterpiece of gigantic confusion can he link this up with tyranny? Confusion is compounded when he identifies Locke as an "empiricist," and Jefferson and Price and Priestley as terrible rationalists, even though Jefferson, Paine, et al. were taking their doctrines squarely from Locke.[16] He

---

[16]Richard Price (1723–1791), a dissenter of Arian convictions, was a great supporter of both American Independence and the French Revolution (it should be noted, however, that he died before the end of the latter). In 1758 he became a minister of the Presbyterian Church in the Newington Green community. He was a member of the Royal Society and of the Pennsylvania Society for Abolishing Negro Slavery. He was also part of numerous intellectual circles; one of his favorites was the Honest Whig club. Price's political philosophy came directly from the moral theory of the autonomy of the individual, according to which an individual, in order to be virtuous, had to be free; and any constraint whatsoever on individual conscience was an arbitrary exercise of power. One of his famous speeches was "On the Love of Our Country," given in 1789 to the Society for the Commemoration of the Glorious Revolution, in which he expressed his unreserved approval for the French Revolution. This speech led

lumps the libertarian Physiocrats together with the tyrant Rousseau. Later on, he praises Jefferson on the U.S. Constitution without fully realizing that the Constitution, which Hayek admires, is precisely an example of systematic rationalist design and the deliberate changing of society.

He points to Bentham as a terrible example of French rationalist influence without pointing out that Bentham was indeed terrible, but why? Precisely because his "rationalism" was a false one, for it rejected and attacked the true rationalist tradition of natural rights. It was because Bentham attacked natural rights and substituted the utilitarian doctrine that morality cannot be found by right reason, that he permitted the State to define morality and employ coercion. Since Hayek doesn't see any significance to natural law or rights, he confuses the whole thing completely.

Burke to publish his *Reflections on the Revolution in France*, and it opened a wide debate on the events in France. Amongst Price's works worthy of note are *A Review of the Principal Questions and Difficulties in Morals* (1758) and *Observations on the Nature of Civil Liberty* (1776).

Joseph Priestley (1733–1804), a prolific writer and innovative thinker, distinguished himself in the fields of theology, political theory, pedagogy, and science. He was a Unitarian, and in 1775 he became minister of the small Presbyterian parish of Needham Market in Suffolk, although his theological stance did not please his parishioners. We later find Priestley teaching literature at the Dissenting Warrington Academy. Then, in 1767, he became a Dissenting minister in Leeds. His attacks on the official Church, his demonstrated support for the French Revolution, and his insistence on the need for parliamentary reform in an age of disorder and fear created the image of Priestley as a threat to order and orthodoxy. This fear led to the Birmingham Riots of 1791 (sometimes referred to as the Priestley Riots). It was during this rioting that Priestley himself, and other Dissenters were attacked, their homes burned, and many of their writings destroyed. In the spring of 1794, he moved to the United States, where he continued his work. He wrote *An Essay on the First Principles of Government* (1768), *Disquisitions Relating to Matter and Spirit* (1777), *Doctrine of Philosophical Necessity* (1777), and *Some Considerations on the Poor in General* (1787). One of the themes of *An Essay on the First Principles of Government* was opposition to any state role in the field of education, in which he thought pluralism and competition should rule.

And, of course, he fails to mention, since it is inconvenient for him, that libertarianism—*laissez-faire*—reached its apogee in the French rationalist works of Bastiat, Molinari, etc., in the middle and late nineteenth century.[17] Bentham erred in being too empirical and pragmatic, just as were Hayek's other heroes, such as Burke. It is ironic that it was

---

[17]Frédéric Bastiat (1801–1850) was orphaned at the age of nine and then raised by relatives. Sometime later he became involved in the family's exporting business. He then went to Spain and Portugal to try, without success, to establish an insurance company. In 1825, he returned to France after inheriting his grandfather's estate. He began his career as a writer, publishing some articles in the *Journal des économistes*. Among these was the "Lettre ouverte à M. de Lamartine sur le droit au travail," a criticism of socialist theories. He was enthusiastic about Richard Cobden's opposition to the Corn Laws in England, about which he wrote *Cobden et la ligue, ou l'Agitation anglaise pour la liberté des échanges*. He published a series of articles in which he attacked protectionism, highlighting the problem of the unintended consequences of government policies. Some of his writings were published in *Sophismes économiques* (1845–1848). In 1846, he founded the Association pour la liberté des échanges in Paris. In addition, because of his writings and speeches he was appointed to the finance commission. Also see his *Harmonies économiques*.

Gustave de Molinari (1819–1912) was one of the most important proponents of *laissez-faire* and liberalism in France. Against protectionism, statism, militarism, colonialism, and socialism, he continued to fight for liberal ideals right up until the eve of the First World War, when he was in his nineties. In 1840, he moved from his native Belgium to Paris to start work as a journalist and economist. His liberalism was based on the theory of natural rights. He supported *laissez-faire* in economics and minimum state intervention in politics. In 1849, in the Journal des économistes, he published "De la production de la sécurité," in which he maintained that private companies working under a regime of competition, along with insurance companies, could supply policing and national security services more efficiently, more economically, and in a more moral way than the state. He contributed a series of articles to the Dictionnaire de l'économie politique (1852–1853). During the reign of Napoleon III, he returned to Belgium where he became a professor of political economy. See also his works *L'Évolution économique du dix-neuvième siècle: théorie du progrès* (1880) and *L'Évolution politique et la révolution* (1884).

Burke who led both the bloody and murderous war against the French abroad and the tyrannical, liberty-destroying suppressions at home—while it was Price and his Radical friends who defended both domestic liberty and foreign isolationism.

Philosophically, Hayek, much as he denies it, is a conservative, in the sense that he believes we must blindly follow traditions even if we can't defend them. He differs from Kirk, et al., largely in a bad way, i.e., by adopting the opposite fallacy that the case for liberty rests on the fact that we know nothing, or very little, and must therefore keep the roads open so that we can learn something. In short, Hayek explicitly rests his case on man's *ignorance*, differing from Kirk who believes that at least tradition gives us some knowledge. This is the J.S. Mill, H.B. Phillips, Gerald Heard argument.[18] Of course, such a puny argument means that, as civilization advances, and we get to know more and more, the case for liberty becomes weaker and weaker. To evade this conclusion, Hayek employs two contradictory stratagems: (1) using the absurd and self-contradictory bromide that "the more we know, the more we know how little we know," and (2) saying even if we do know more, we still know less than we don't know, i.e., we still know less than 50 percent of what there is to be known. How he *knows* this is, of course, in the lap of the gods.

Both the Kirkian worship of the past and the Mill-Phillips emphasis on man's ignorance have one thing in common: their attack on man's reason. But how else could Hayek combine two contradictory fallacies? In an interesting way: through his knowledge of the free market. For to Hayek, the market is an example of a social institution that works better than any individual knows and is needed because of each

---

[18]Gerald Heard (1889–1971). A historian and philosopher, Heard studied at Cambridge and briefly taught at Oxford before moving in 1937 to the United States. He briefly taught at Duke University before founding Trabuco College in 1941. He was well known for his evolutionary theory of human consciousness. See his works *The Ascent of Humanity* (1929), *The Source of Civilization* (1935), and *The Five Ages of Man* (1963).

person's ignorance. But while subtle, this too is a fallacious argument. For there is nothing really mysterious about the market: the fact that Hayek can explain its workings shows that reason can comprehend it; and since every single transaction benefits both parties and rewards rationality, it is not surprising that the *sum* of all market transactions is a beautiful and rational instrument. In short, if irrational entrepreneurs lose money and rational ones make profits, it is not surprising that a profit-run economy will be rational.

To deprecate human reason by saying that none of us is or can be omniscient is absurd, for it takes an impossible standard as the judge of a possible and real condition. All of our knowledge we get from the exercise of our reason; to say that no man can be God and know everything is to take an irrational standard of evaluation.

There are countless other examples of tortuous fallacies—for example, Hayek's *denial* that a free market allocates income in accordance with merit. Here he tries to make a vague and absurd distinction between "merit" and "value," and, of course, his denial plays into the hands of the egalitarians. For Hayek attacks the very idea that justice can be known by man or that it could be applied, and says, see, since we can't be just and reward according to merit, you'd better accept the free market. Will a man thirsting for justice accept this dictum—or that of the socialists, who promise him justice and reason? In fact, Hayek, almost incredibly, seems to identify *merit* with *pain*; if somebody enjoys achieving something, he is not meritorious, but if he suffered while doing so, then he is meritorious. To take pain as one's standard of the good is hair-raising indeed.

On democracy, Hayek is again confused; he begins by separating liberalism neatly from democracy and finally ends by confusing them, talking of democracy as also a good, etc.

Finally, even on his revered rule of law, equality under general rules, which Hayek establishes to the exclusion of more important contentual doctrines of liberty, Hayek backtracks so much as even to eradicate *that*. First, he upholds the von Gneist[19] thesis of "administrative courts" as being competent to exercise judicial review of administrative agencies; in thus throwing over the jurisdiction of ordinary courts on the ground that these courts wouldn't be expert enough to judge, Hayek in effect throws over the rule of law and accepts administrative tyranny. For the *reason* why ordinary courts should rule is precisely that they can be governed by a common libertarian law: that the government should not infringe on liberty and property; the fact that some other courts are to be set up on some *other* basis concedes the essence of the struggle to administrative discretion. Further, Hayek also concedes that his rule of law should be breached in war or other serious emergencies, and even concedes that this vaunted rule cannot be meaningfully defined.

I have not yet seen Hayek's final chapters on specific economic applications, but I can predict that I will have plenty to complain about there. In the light of this book, we cannot simply continue to regard F.A. Hayek as a good fellow who is against coercion, and against egalitarianism, and favors a reasonable amount of freedom. For any good aspects are far overshadowed by his predominant tone, which is this:

> We must accept traditional social institutions on blind faith and without adequate reason; reason is impotent to discover moral principles or justice, but to the extent that we can discover merit it is based on pain, and the free market must violate it; the argument for freedom rests on ignorance; this freedom really means equality under the law, which means general, predictable rules, whatever their content; *laissez-faire* is bad because it is wicked and extreme and tyrannical French rationalism—

---

[19]Rudolf von Gneist (1816–1895) was a German jurist and liberal politician. He was the author of fundamental works on English constitutional and administrative law. He had a particularly important role in the reform of the Prussian administration (1868–1875) and in building an autonomous admintrative justice system in Germany. See D*as heutige englische Verfassungs- und Verwaltungsrecht* (1857) and *Englische Verfassungsgeschichte* (1882).

our proper course is to employ general rules, but
to find these rules only in empirical, pragmatic,
one-step-at-a-time fashion—and we must follow
these rules except where emergencies present
themselves.

And a further point: Hayek rests his case for his principles not on individual rights or welfare, but on "social" considerations: society is better off if some people discover
things, etc. So that *individual* "liberty" is only a grant from
society.

This then, is the face that F.A. Hayek will present to the
world in his *Constitution of Liberty*. It is a face such that, if
I were a young man first getting interested in political questions, and I should read *this* as the best product of the
"extreme Right," I would become a roaring leftist in no
time, and so I believe would almost anyone. That is why I
consider this such a dangerous book and why I believe that
right-wingers should attack this book with great vigor when
it appears, instead of what I am sure they will do: applaud
it like so many trained seals. For (1) Hayek attacks *laissez-
faire* and attacks or ignores the true libertarians, thus setting up the "even Hayek admits . . ." line; and (2) his argument is based on a deprecation or dismissal of both reason
and justice, so that anyone interested in reason or justice
would tend to oppose the whole book. And because of
Hayek's great prominence in the intellectual world, any failure by extreme right-wingers to attack the book with the
implacable vigor it deserves will inordinately harm the right-
wing cause that we all hold dear.

Such are the partisan biases that stem from Hayek's lack
of sound principle, and which vitiate, and more than offset,
the various good passages and sections in the economic sections of the book.

Cordially,

Murray

3.

LETTER ON
THE CONSTITUTION OF LIBERTY BY F.A. HAYEK

June 11, 1960
Mr. Kenneth S. Templeton
William Volker Fund

Dear Ken:

F.A. Hayek's *The Constitution of Liberty* is a work monumental in its scope and invaluable for the extent of its erudition.[20] Of the twenty-five chapters in the complete work, I reviewed fourteen in detail in draft form. (See my confidential memorandum of January 21, 1958, and my critique for Hayek sent to you on January 24, 1958.) The major change in those chapters is the far greater breadth of the footnotes, which now become an invaluable reference source for people wishing to dig further into the literature on liberty.

Hayek's work may be divided into three parts: philosophical, historical, and economic applications. His aim is to erect a groundwork for a theory and systematic approach to liberty; unfortunately Hayek fails in this aim, in all three departments.

Philosophically, Hayek grounds freedom solely on the shaky reed of man's ignorance. There are good arguments to be drawn for leaving all roads open so that knowledge can expand, but this hardly deserves the exclusive reliance that Hayek places on it. So concerned is Hayek to oppose rationalism as the threat to liberty, that he abandons any attempt

---

[20]F.A. Hayek, *The Constitution of Liberty* (Chicago: University of Chicago Press, 1960).

for a rationalist groundwork *for* liberty. While Hayek has improved on his previous draft slightly, in richness of material and in qualifying particularly poor passages, there is no substantive change in his position. As before, Hayek begins very well in the first chapter by defining freedom as meaning "absence of coercion," but fails badly in defining "coercion." For Hayek, "coercion" is defined as arbitrary, specifically harmful acts; the term is thus used much more broadly and yet more narrowly than its proper definition: "the use of violence." Hence, Hayek can say that for a factory to fire a worker in a place where unemployment is heavy—or to threaten to fire him—is an act of "coercion," on the same level as actual acts of violence.

Hayek's only principle of noncoercion for government is the "rule of law," on which he places exclusive reliance. In such a chapter as chapter 16, "The Decline of the Law," Hayek is excellent in attacking modern legal philosophers who push the state in a socialistic direction beyond the rule: such as Kelsen and the legal positivists, and Harold Laski.[21] However, Hayek spends virtually equal emphasis on attacking those who would narrow the rule to limit government activity to defense of life, liberty, and property. Hayek attacks this as an "extreme," unduly narrow, etc., view of the role of government. To Hayek, *laissez-faire* is almost as bad an outgrowth of "rationalism" as is socialism.

This book makes clear to me, as the first fourteen chapters of the draft did not, that Hayek's rule of law limits are

---

[21]Harold Laski (1893–1950) was an English political theorist and professor of political science at the London School of Economics from 1926 to 1950. He was convinced that socialism in England had been more greatly influenced by John Stuart Mill than by Karl Marx, and he taught a kind of modified Marxism. He was a member of the Labour Party's National Executive Committee between 1937 and 1949 and significantly influenced its policy. He was chairman of the Labour Party from 1945 to 1946. He wrote *A Grammar of Politics* (1925); *Liberty in the Modern State* (1930); *Reflections on the Revolution of Our Time* (1943); and *The American Democracy* (1948).

even looser than I had thought. For not only does he admit at one point that the rule of law cannot be precisely defined, and that it must be suspended in emergencies, but he also would only apply the rule to what Hayek calls "coercive" activities of the State. There is a vast area of State activity which Hayek calls "noncoercive" and where the State can act perfectly legitimately. "Coercive" activities are thus confined to such direct acts of tyranny as price controls, fixing production, socialist planning, etc. But a government supply of a service—such as public housing, etc.—is *not* considered coercive, and therefore *cannot* be opposed on principle according to Hayek. For such "noncoercive" activities, says Hayek, the proposed activity must be considered case by case, *ad hoc*, in a pragmatic, utilitarian manner.

Furthermore, even such clearly coercive activities of the government as conscription are not considered really coercive by Hayek because they are general rules, applying to everyone in a certain defined category (although, as Hayek sometimes admits, these categories can be widened and narrowed flexibly). Everyone *knows* in advance that he will be drafted, he can predict it, etc. (Of course, in practice, the draft is neither universal nor predictable, but that is another problem.)

Hayek's devotion to the *relatively* unimportant rule of law principle, and his hostility to rationalism, distort his historical sections so as to make them virtually valueless (although, as I said above, the footnote references are most important). Thus, Hayek tries to erect the categories of the "English tradition" (good) and the "French tradition" (bad). Jefferson, Paine, Price, etc.—fine libertarians all—are dismissed hostilely as being in the bad French tradition, while their direct ancestor, John Locke, is hailed as a "good" English empiricist. Actually, there was little difference between them. Condorcet, surely a "bad" French rationalist by Hayek's standards, somehow comes out "good" because he favored a constitution for France and is therefore supposed to be in favor of the rule of law. And while favoring the American Constitution, the Bill of

Rights, and the Ninth Amendment as defending liberty, Hayek erroneously considers the American Revolution to be really conservative, and far worse, defends the New Deal Supreme Court for correcting the "extreme" views of the Old Supreme Court in outlawing interventionary measures, etc.

Most grievous omission of all, for a historical discussion of libertarian thought, is the complete failure to discuss the really libertarian French thinkers of the nineteenth century: Bastiat, Molinari, Dunoyer, etc.[22] For these rationalist, pure libertarians would have revealed Hayek's error in identifying rationalism and tyranny, and in placing such faith in the eighteenth-century English Old Whigs. Even the nineteenth-century classical economists of England are too "French" for Hayek's taste, although it is impossible to see how Benthamite utilitarianism can be "French"; it was original with Bentham. Hayek's unfortunate "rationalist French" vs. "Whiggish British" traditions, makes him neglect all the really important problems in a history of libertarian thought: e.g., the split between the natural-rights and the utilitarian traditions of liberty. Both of these schools of thought are virtually ignored.

This book is thus a tragic failure, despite the many profound passages scattered through the book, despite the wealth of references, and despite the isolated chapters that have much net value (these are chapter 1, defining liberty

---

[22]Charles Dunoyer (1786–1862) studied law in Paris where he was intellectually tied to Charles Comte. In 1814, together with Comte, he founded the journal Le Censeur, which was then banned by the emperor. Dunoyer was condemned to a year in prison and banned from Paris for five years. From Vitré, he published *Le Censeur européen* intermittently until 1820. He was opposed to the Bourbon restoration and supported absolute freedom in politics and in social and economic life. He was convinced that the industrial system would develop without any intervention on the part of the state. Among Dunoyer's works, see *Nouveau traité d'économie sociale* (1830) and *L'industrie et la morale considérées dans leur rapports avec la liberté* (1825).

and attacking the socialistic definitions; chapter 8, on employment, independence, and the role of the intellectuals; chapter 16, on the modern decline of the rule of law; chapter 20, which, though advocating fallacious proportional taxation, is valuable on balance for its fine criticisms of progressive taxation; and the postscript, which has much keen critique of "conservatism," although its positive position is a weak, ultimately pragmatic "Whiggism").

It is, in fine, a tragic failure because, setting out in this big book to establish a groundwork and a system for liberty, this is precisely what Hayek fails to do and which constitutes his chief error. He has no principle for liberty. His only principle is the "rule of law," and this, weak anyway, is so vitiated and qualified that, by the end, there is virtually no principle remaining.

This lack of principle can best be shown by a list I have compiled from the book, setting forth Hayek's partisan biases, biases stemming from his odd concept of the State's "noncoercive" activities, and from his defining "coercion" peculiarly to include "neighborhood effects" on others' property, etc. The following is the list of Hayek's specific partisan biases in economic applications of his theory.

Hayek favors the following:

- requiring "monopolist" not to discriminate in price among his customers
- government sanitation
- government roads
- compulsory jury service (which he considers "noncoercive")
- compulsory deputizing of constables (also, as I've said, conscription is "noncoercive")
- government enforcement of religious conformity *in an age* when people believe that the collective community is responsible for everyone's actions against God (e.g., if people believe that homosexuals would bring down the wrath of Sodom and Gomorrah upon them, homosexuality should be outlawed)
- government enforcement of "rules of conduct" in public places (a vague endorsement)

- suspension of liberty in "emergencies" (e.g., the right of habeas corpus), in the "public interest"
- the "clear and present danger" invasion of free speech
- government subsidies in the "public interest" (e.g., for "defense")
- government supplying of a monetary system
- government supplying of standards weights and measures
- government supplying of statistics
- government surveying
- government sanitary services
- government health services
- municipal services
- government public works—which individuals would not pay for
- many government enterprises, so long as they are not compulsorily "monopolistic"
- "factory" acts, and other government regulations of production
- interference with absolute private property in land
- failure of government to enforce gambling contracts
- government aid to the indigent, up to a "minimum of subsistence" for everyone; *and* this "minimum" keeps rising along with the general standard of living(!)
- government subsidies for scientific research, other "experiments"
- municipal government parks
- municipal government museums
- municipal government theaters
- municipal government sports facilities
- outlawing of peaceful secondary strikes and boycotts
- collective bargaining, on work rules—which Hayek fails completely to realize are hindrances on production and on management's private property, and which he identifies as extensions of the rule of law to industry(!?)
- collective barganing on wage differentials (Note: collective bargaining should not be outlawed, but an economist should realize its economic evils and its lack of advantages)

- outlawing of voluntary closed-shop "yellow-dog" contracts

- compulsory old-age insurance

- compulsory unemployment insurance; Hayek favors Federal compulsion on everyone to take out insurance, rather than for the government to "insure" everyone directly itself; however, he would supplement this with "temporary" federal aid and subsidy to private insurance companies for such insurance (all this he would do along the lines of existing compulsory automobile insurance, which he also favors)

Further, while opposed to the existing federal social security program, Hayek is *against* scrapping it entirely, now that it is set up, and only favors a gradual transformation of the present system into his proposed system.

Hayek is also *against* a monetary policy so "tight" as to lead to protracted unemployment (even though he sees that unions would be responsible for this unemployment).

- an odd maximum limit on proportional taxation which would only be the percentage of national income extracted by the government; thus, if the government decides to extract 50 percent of the national income, his proposed maximum would be 50 percent

Hayek favors central banking and is opposed to a free-market money.

He is *against* the return to a gold standard; instead he favors governmental stabilization of the price level, including in such measures a "commodity reserve standard."

Hayek also believes that absolute private-property rights are *invalid* in cities, and advocates larger municipal ownership.

He favors the following:

- town planning by government, to coordinate neighborhoods, etc.

- town planners

    a. taxing property owners who "gain" by their measures even though the individual property owner may be opposed to the measure

    b. subsidizing the "losers"

- the right of *expropriation* of private property by government (right of eminent domain, etc.) provided it is at "fair compensation"—the "fair compensation," of course to be determined by . . . government

He *concedes* that the Henry George single-tax plan would be fine if only there could be clearly separated in practice the site value from the improvement value of land;

He favors

- governmental building codes, and minimum safety regulation

- compulsory expropriation of land

- federal government parks, and "nature reservations"

- federal government spreading of agricultural knowledge to farmers

- compulsory minimum education for children, with government of course setting the minimum standards

- government aid for education of the poor; he seems to adopt the Friedman plan for government financing of every parent, who can choose his own private school, thus eliminating the need for public schools (of course, the private schools would have to meet governmental "minimum standards"); however, he *doesn't go as far* as the Friedman plan, because Hayek

  a. wants to retain public schools in isolated districts where private schools would not pay

  b. in retrospect, favors public schools for nineteenth-century America, when transportation was poorer, and where public schools were needed to "Americanize" the immigrants compulsorily

- "academic freedom" and "tenure" in colleges

- government, federal aid to higher education especially of general scientists and scholars

- government special taxation of slum property

Cordially,

Murray

4.

REVIEW OF LIONEL ROBBINS, *THE GREAT DEPRESSION*

November 14, 1959
Dr. Ivan R. Bierly
William Volker Fund

Dear Ivan:

Lionel Robbins's *The Great Depression*[23] is one of the great economic works of our time. Its greatness lies not so much in originality of economic thought, as in the application of the best economic thought to the explanation of the cataclysmic phenomena of the Great Depression. This is unquestionably the best work published on the Great Depression.

At the time that Robbins wrote this work, he was perhaps the second most eminent follower of Ludwig von Mises (Hayek being the first). To his work, Robbins brought a clarity and polish of style that I believe to be unequalled among any economists, past or present. Robbins is the premier economic stylist.

In this brief, clear, but extremely meaty book, Robbins sets forth first the Misesian theory of business cycles and then applies it to the events of the 1920s and 1930s. We see how bank credit expansion in the United States, Great Britain, and other countries (in Britain generated because of the rigid wage structure caused by unions and the unemployment insurance system, as well as a return to the gold standard at too high a par; and in the United States generated

---

[23]Lionel Robbins, *The Great Depression* (London: Macmillan, 1934).

by a desire to inflate in order to help Britain as well as an absurd devotion to the ideal of a stable price level) drove the civilized world into a great depression.

Then Robbins shows how the various nations took measures to counteract and cushion the depression that could only make it worse: propping up unsound, shaky business positions; inflating credit; expanding public works; keeping up wage rates (e.g., Hoover and his White House conferences)—all things that prolonged the necessary depression adjustments and profoundly aggravated the catastrophe. Robbins is particularly bitter about the wave of tariffs, exchange controls, quotas, etc., that prolonged crises, set nation against nation, and fragmented the international division of labor.

And this is not all. Robbins also sets the European scene in the context of the disruptions of the largely free market brought about by World War I; the statization, unionization, and cartelization of the economy that the war brought about; the dislocation of industrial investment and agricultural over-production brought about by war demand, etc. And above all, the gold standard of pre-World War I, that truly international money, was disrupted and never really brought back again. Robbins shows the tragedy of this, and defends the gold standard vigorously against charges that it "broke down" in 1929. He shows that the U.S. inflation in 1927 and 1928 when it was losing gold, and Britain's cavalierly going off gold when its bank discount rate was as low as 4.5 percent, was in flagrant violation of the "rules" of the gold standard (as was Britain's persistent inflationism in the 1920s).

Robbins also has excellent sections demonstrating the Misesian point that one intervention leads inexorably to another intervention or else repeal of the original policy. He also has a critique of the idea of central planning and a fine summation of the Misesian demonstration that socialist economies cannot calculate. Almost every important relevant point is touched upon and handled in unexceptionable fashion. Thus, Robbins, touching on the monopoly question, shows that the only really important monopolies are those created and fostered by governments. He has not the time for a rigorous demonstration of this, but his *apercus* are important, stimulating, and sound. Robbins sums up his book in this superb passage:

> It has been the object . . . to show that if recovery is to be maintained and future progress assured, there must be a more or less complete reversal of contemporary tendencies of governmental regulation of enterprise. The aim of governmental policy in regard to industry must be to create a field in which the forces of enterprise and the disposal of resources are once more allowed to be governed by the market.
>
> But what is this but the restoration of capitalism? And is not the restoration of capitalism the restoration of the causes of depression?
>
> If the analysis of this essay is correct, the answer is unequivocal. The conditions of recovery which have been stated do indeed involve the restoration of what has been called capitalism. But the slump was not due to these conditions. On the contrary, it was due to their negation. It was due to monetary mismanagement and State intervention operating in a milieu in which the essential strength of capitalism had already been sapped by war and by policy. Ever since the outbreak of war in 1914, the whole tendency of policy has been away from that system, which in spite of the persistence of feudal obstacles and the unprecedented multiplication of the people, produced that enormous increase of wealth per head. . . . Whether that increase will be resumed, or whether, after perhaps some recovery, we shall be plunged anew into depression and the chaos of planning and restrictionism—that is the issue which depends on our willingness to reverse this tendency.[24]

The Great Depression, in short, is a brilliant work that should be read by every economist. It is not at all outdated.

---

[24]Ibid., pp. 213–14.

It deserves the widest possible distribution, and would be indeed a fitting companion to Hazlitt's *The Fallacies of the New Economics*, that refutation of the other great explanation of the Depression—the Keynesian.

Cordially,

Murray

5.

LETTER ON
THE EIGHTEENTH-CENTURY COMMONWEALTHMAN
BY CAROLINE ROBBINS

November 26, 1959
Mr. Kenneth S. Templeton
William Volker Fund

Dear Ken:

Caroline Robbins's *The Eighteenth-Century Commonwealthman*, which you asked me to report upon when I saw you last in New York, is a monumental book.[25] (Its subtitle is "Studies in the Transmission, Development, and Circumstance of English Liberal Thought from the Restoration of Charles II until the War with the Thirteen Colonies.") To students of the liberal tradition and its history ("liberal" in

---

[25]Caroline Robbins, *The Eighteenth Century Commonwealthman: Studies in the Transmission, Development, and Circumstance of English Liberal Thought from the Restoration of Charles II until the War with the Thirteen Colonies* (Cambridge, Mass.: Harvard University Press, 1959).

the old-fashioned sense of a believer in liberty), there has always been a great gap: what happened between the days of Locke and the Revolution of 1688, and the Wilkes agitation in the 1760s in Britain? How is it possible that, as it seems, the libertarian viewpoint completely died out after 1688, only to spring up, lively and almost full-grown, in the 1760s and 1770s? This conclusion seemed impossible, and yet no one knew anything about the great gap between the end of the seventeenth century and the last quarter of the eighteenth. It seemed as if no liberals existed during that entire period to bridge the gap.

Well, now Professor Caroline Robbins, sister of the economist Lionel Robbins and Professor at Bryn Mawr College, has filled in this gap in one of the most impressive feats of scholarship I have seen in a long while. For what Miss Robbins had to do was to plow almost totally virgin soil, in very obscure primary sources such as pamphlets, diaries, etc., of the period, there being virtually no secondary sources on the entire period. In her footnotes there are virtually no references after about 1800.

Caroline Robbins has unearthed the liberals of this whole epoch, and extensively traced the influences and interconnections. They are certainly not as great as Locke, whom she treats in the introductory chapter of the work, or the magnificent Price, whom she treats in a fascinating final chapter, but they are important enough, and they are all unearthed and given their role in the procession. In her packed pages will be found a discussion of the excellent magazine the Old Whig; of that grand old man of liberty, Thomas Hollis—the Pierre Goodrich of his era—who played a considerable role in fomenting the American Revolution by collecting and disseminating and reprinting libertarian books and pamphlets all over the world, especially in America.[26] His was perhaps

---

[26]Thomas Hollis (1720–1774) made a fundamental contribution to the recovery of the republican tradition in the seventeenth century. A great reader and freethinker, he devoted himself to the republication of the works of Harrington, Milton, Nedham, Sidney, and Locke.

the first "Liberty Library." Here are found the various important "circles" of friends that helped to foster and carry on the liberal gospel in an era of ignorant stand-pattery.

In the early eighteenth century, the leader of the liberal group was one Robert Molesworth, resurrected from almost complete obscurity.[27] Molesworth's own ideas weren't particularly good, but he performed the important function of heading and nourishing a circle of friends and acquaintances who carried on the great tradition, albeit watered down a bit, of Locke and Sidney. Other interesting figures are James Foster, the Scot Dr. John Campbell, James Burgh, John Jackson, and John Lee.[28] Another grand "leader of the circle was the

---

In 1960, Pierre Goodrich founded the Liberty Fund, a private organization for the dissemination of classical-liberal ideas.

[27]Robert Molesworth (1656–1725) supported William of Orange on the occasion of the Glorious Revolution and, in 1695, became a member of the Irish Privy Council. He was made a viscount in 1716. He wrote *An Account of Denmark as It Was in the Year 1692* (1693).

[28]James Foster (1697–1748), a keen collaborator on the liberal paper *The Old Whig*, was a Dissenting chaplain in the house of Robert Houlton. In 1724 he moved to London where he became a famous nonconformist preacher of liberal ideas. His thought was characterized by an emphasis on the dignity and freedom of the individual, and on freedom of thought. His speeches were published in *Discourses* (1749–1752) and in *Sermons* (1736).

John Campbell (1653–1728) was a Scot who immigrated to Boston, where he published the *Boston Newsletter*, helping to disseminate English liberal ideas in the colonies.

Between 1774 and 1775, James Burgh (1714–1775) published *Political Disquisitions*, one of the political tracts that significantly influenced radical thought in the 1780s. See Burgh, *Political Disquisitions; or, An Enquiry into Public Errors, Defects, and Abuses*, 3 vols. (London: E. and C. Dilly, 1774–75). Looking at the first part of the eighteenth century, Burgh regretted the degeneration of the country and with the "spirit of a true independent whig," he hoped for the restoration of the constitution to control the authoritarian tendencies of the government (General Preface, p. xvi). He wrote,

> All lawful authority, legislative, and executive, origi-
> nates from the people. Power in the people is like

radical Anglican Archdeacon Blackburne.[29] Francis Hutcheson[30] is shown to have played a very important role, in England as well as Scotland, and is shown to be a far better libertarian than his pupil, Adam Smith. (Although there is a

---

light in the sun, native, original, inherent, and unlim-
ited by anything human. In governors, it may be com-
pared to the reflected light of the moon, for it is only
borrowed, delegated, and limited by the intention of
the people, whose it is, and to whom governors are to
consider themselves responsible, while the people are
answerable only to God.

Central to Burgh's thought was his criticism of the electoral system, which he considered to be corrupt and unrepresentative. Burgh
wanted the right to vote to be extended to all those who paid taxes,
because only in this way could the balance in favor of the great
landowners be redressed and trade and manufacturing interests be
represented. It is worth noting that Burgh advocated extending the
right to vote to anyone who paid taxes—he was not talking about
universal male suffrage. While maintaining the need for wider representation, Burgh did not question the link between property and
political representation.

John Jackson (1686–1763) wrote *The Grounds of Civil and
Ecclesiastical Government*, in which he maintained that the state
should be limited by natural law and the resulting civil laws. Jackson
criticized the theory of the divine right of kings and maintained that
the citizens were bound to the sovereign as long as the sovereign
acted justly; otherwise the power was dissolved.

John Lee (1733–1793) was part of the circle of Rational Dissenters and a member of the Club of Honest Whigs together with
Price and Burgh. A friend of Joseph Priestley, he was solicitor general in the Rockingham administration.

[29]Francis Blackburne (1705–1787) published *The Confessional*
(1766) anonymously in defense of the Unitarian faith and against the
restrictions imposed on religious dissenters.

[30]Francis Hutcheson (1694–1746) was considered to be one of the
main exponents of the Scottish Enlightenment. In 1729, he succeeded
Gershom Carmichael (see note below) in the chair of moral philosophy
at the University of Glasgow, and Adam Smith was one of his students.
Hutcheson placed at the basis of any moral judgment a feeling grounded
in the notion that human nature produced approval for virtuous actions
and disapproval for vicious actions. This instinct explained the possibility of moral judgments independent of any considerations dictated by

curious neglect of Hutcheson's teacher, Gershom Carmichael.[31]) And later on, we see how these influences tie in with the later "radical" libertarians, such as Earl Stanhope, Major John Cartwright, John Jebb, Capel Lofft, and the great Richard Price.[32]

---

immediate interest, i.e., judgments formulated in view of the public good. Hutcheson thought that it was the right of any individual to enjoy the fruits of his own labor and therefore that society had to guarantee private property in the public interest. An equally important idea of his was the division of labor as a form of cooperation. Among his works, see *An Inquiry Concerning the Origin of Our Ideas of Virtue or Moral Good* (1725) and *A System of Moral Philosophy* (1755).

[31]Gershom Carmichael (c. 1672–1729) was an early figure in the Scottish Enlightenment. After his studies at the University of Edinburgh, he became rector at the University of St. Andrews and later at the University of Glasgow. Then, in 1727, he became the first professor of moral philosophy at Glasgow. He inaugurated the teaching of economics and introduced into Scotland the study of the theorists of natural law, including Grotius and Pufendorf. As an assigned text, he employed *De officio hominis et civis* by Pufendorf, editing two editions, one in 1718 and another in 1724. In his comments, Carmichael gave ample attention to economic questions relating to money, prices, and taxes, in particular supporting the theory that it was the scarcity of a good that determined its value.

[32]Charles Stanhope (1753–1816) supported the campaign for parliamentary reform, the extension of suffrage, and the abolition of discriminatory laws against religious dissenters. He joined forces with radicals such as Jebb and Cartwright. He was known for his republican ideas, and sympathized with both the American and French Revolutions.

John Cartwright (1740–1824) was part of the movement of radicals and dissenters in favor of parliamentary reform. The aims of the movement were the abolition of the Test Act and the Corporation Act, which, by requiring religious conformism for those in public office, were in practice discriminatory laws against religious dissenters. At the center of the debate on the reforms were the extension of suffrage, an increase in the frequency of elections, and the abolition of the so-called "rotten boroughs." The reform campaign was led by Charles James Fox from inside Parliament, and by Christopher Wyvill and Cartwright from the outside. Cartwright, in 1776, published the famous *Take Your Choice!* His main ideas were the introduction of universal male suffrage, the secret ballot, annual elections, and equality among electoral districts. He influenced radical thought in

We see the interesting and important roles played in maintaining and fostering the liberal tradition by the dissenters, by Yorkshiremen, by the Anglo-Irish seeking relaxation of English bonds, by Cambridge University and by the dissenting Academies of the West Country. We see the importance, in the early period, of Trenchard and Gordon, authors of the *Cato* letters.[33] And we find such intriguing characters as

---

the first half of the nineteenth century. Cartwright's influence was evident in the six points of the Chartists, a sociopolitical movement that developed in England between 1838 and 1850 that aimed to improve the terrible conditions of the working class and to introduce, at the political level, such fundamental rights as universal suffrage.

John Jebb (1736–1786) was a Unitarian who studied at Trinity College. He taught mathematics, but various colleges prohibited their students from attending his lectures because of his nonconformist religious ideas. He was in favor of independence for the American colonies and he condemned English policy towards America.

Capel Lofft (1751–1824) joined the radical movement for parliamentary reform in the second half of the eighteenth century. He was the author of *An Argument on the Nature of Party and Faction: In Which Is Considered the Duty of a Good and Peaceable Citizen at the Present Crisis* (1780).

[33]John Trenchard (1662–1723), a political writer and polemicist, was known for, among other things, his writings against a standing army. He was elected to Parliament and in 1719 he began to work with Thomas Gordon, with whom he published *Cato's Letters* in the *London Journal* from 1719 to 1723. This was a series of articles criticizing government activities in general. Among his works, see *A Short History of Standing Armies in England* (1698).

Thomas Gordon (c. 1692–1750) was a lawyer in Scotland who later moved to London, where he began his work as a political writer and polemicist. Among Gordon's works, see *The Conspirators, The Case of Catiline* (1721); *A Learned Dissertation Upon Old Women* (1720); *Three Political Letters to a Noble Lord, Concerning Liberty and Constitution* (1721).

Trenchard and Gordon helped to disseminate the thought of Locke, applying his ideas to the concrete problems of the government of the day. Their most important writings, in this regard, were *Cato's Letters*, which came out in various editions in the American colonies where they were widely distributed. It seems that they were very important in forging the theoretical basis for the American Revolution. Gordon and Trenchard gave a particularly radical turn to Locke's thought. While

Thomas Bradbury,[34] who celebrated publicly at the death of Queen Anne, and of Sylas Neville, who always feasted and celebrated at the anniversary of the execution of Charles I, and denounced that "dog, George III."[35] And we are touched to find that William Pitt the Elder, a fair-weather friend of many of the true liberals, was snubbed by them for years for "selling out" by accepting the title of Earl of Chatham.[36] And we also find that many leading literary figures of the eighteenth century were quite close to the liberals, including Jonathan Swift, Henry Fielding, William Hazlitt, and James Boswell.[37]

Locke justified rebelling against the government when the latter violated the natural rights of individuals, the two authors maintained that the government always tended to destroy individual rights rather than protect them. According to *Cato's Letters*, the history of mankind was none other than the history of conflict between power and freedom. Power, i.e., the state, was always ready to violate the rights of its citizens and take away their freedom; therefore the state should be reduced to the minimum and be constantly controlled. See John Trenchard and Thomas Gordon, *Cato's Letters*, in *The English Libertarian Heritage: From the Writings of John Trenchard and Thomas Gordon in the Independent Whig and Cato's Letters*, ed. David L. Jacobson (San Francisco, Calif.: Fox and Wilkes, 1994). Gordon and Trenchard also published *The Character of an Independent Whig* (London: J. Roberts, 1719–1720).

[34]Thomas Bradbury (1677–1759) congregationalist dissenter, known for the polemic content of his political writings.

[35]Sylas Neville (1741–1840) kept a diary that is useful in understanding the thought and politics of the republicans in the first twenty years of the reign of George III. See *The Diary of Sylas Neville, 1767–1788*.

[36]William Pitt (1708–1778) was a famous English statesman and, from 1766, the first Earl of Chatham. He played a frontline role in the Seven Years War (1756–63), which ensured the transformation of England into an imperial power. He opposed the Treaty of Paris (1763), which concluded the war.

[37]Jonathan Swift (1667–1745) was an Irish writer and politician, first politically on the side of the Whigs and then of the Tories. In reality, he was more of an Old Whig, defending traditional English freedoms and rights although he feared democratic and egalitarian offshoots. In *Gulliver's Travels* (1726), he described the

There are a few difficulties with the book. Perhaps the main one is that Miss Robbins is sometimes wobbly about whom she should admit to the liberal pantheon, and that she lets in quite a few people who are not liberals even by a generous stretch of the imagination. Her standards are unfortunately not high enough, and this is particularly true in the chapter on Scotland, where she includes Robert Wallace, who was practically a communist, as well as quite unliberal people like Adam Ferguson.[38] She includes land communists

---

paradox of a kind of ethics and politics following nature and reason, applying them in the kingdom of the philosopher horses and another kingdom based on injustice and the abuse of men reduced to slaves.

Henry Fielding (1707–1754) was an English novelist and playwright who wrote *Joseph Andrews* (1742) and *Tom Jones* (1749).

William Hazlitt (1778–1830) was an English writer of Unitarian origins and a friend of William Wordsworth, Samuel Taylor Coleridge, Percy Bysshe Shelly, and John Keats. Author of *An Essay on the Principles of Human Action* (1805), he worked for the *Morning Chronicle*, and his articles appeared in the collection *A View of the English Stage* (1818). See, among others, *Characters of Shakespeare's Plays* (1817) and *The Spirit of the Age* (1825).

James Boswell (1749–1795), a Scottish lawyer, attended Adam Smith's lectures at Glasgow University. During a trip to Europe in 1764, he interviewed Rousseau and Voltaire. He is most well known as the biographer of the famous man of letters Samuel Johnson, *The Life of Samuel Johnson* (1791).

[38]Robert Wallace (1697–1771), a Scottish Presbyterian minister, was the author of *Various Prospects of Mankind, Nature and Providence* (1761), a communitarian utopia. In this work, Wallace described the idea of a world government that eliminated private property and imposed equality. In his ideal world, the raising of children would be delegated to the state.

Adam Ferguson (1723–1816), a Scottish philosopher and historian, taught moral philosophy at the University of Edinburgh from 1764 to 1785. He was one of the most important figures of the Scottish Enlightenment. Author of *An Essay on the History of Civil Society* (1767), he was one of the exponents of the spontaneous order tradition. According to Ferguson,

like William Ogilvie[39] and Thomas Spence, and she is especially fond of a statist character like Thomas Pownall.[40] In
short, while she is obviously extremely sympathetic with the

> Like the winds that come we know not whence, and blow
> whithersoever they list, the forms of society are derived
> from an obscure and distant origin; they arise, long
> before the date of philosophy, from the instincts, not
> from the speculations of men. . . . This is the simplest
> form under which we can consider the establishment of
> nations: and we ascribe to a previous design, what
> came to be known only by experience, what no human
> wisdom could foresee, and what, without the concur-
> ring humour and disposition of his age, no authority
> could enable an individual to execute. (*An Essay on
> the History of Civil Society* [Whitefish, Mont.:
> Kessinger Publishing, 2004], pp. 75–76)

One of the characteristic aspects of his thought was a profound
criticism of commercial society, which, he claimed, through the division of labor, alienated man, depriving him of his humanity. For Ferguson, the development of the mechanical arts and the growth of
production and trade did not automatically lead to moral and political progress. The division of labor in the sphere of the state, furthermore, had led to the establishment of a standing army that, in
Ferguson's opinion, was yet another instrument of oppression in the
hands of government. Ferguson therefore proposed the republican
ideal of the citizen soldier. This explicitly recalled the values and
ideas of the modern republican tradition. He thought that freedom
could be kept alive not so much by constitutions and laws but rather
by the active participation of citizens in civil life.

[39]William Ogilvie (1736–1819) taught philosophy at the Aberdeen
University and was a supporter of the theory of the joint property of
the earth.

[40]Thomas Spence (1750–1814), an English radical, maintained
that all land should be public. In 1792 he moved to London where
he earned his living selling copies of *The Rights of Man* by Thomas
Paine on street corners. He was arrested on several occasions for
distributing seditious texts. In 1793, for a short time, he published
the journal *Pig's Meat*. He opened a shop selling books with radical
ideas. He supported women's rights.

Thomas Pownall (1722–1805) was the author of *Administration
of the Colonies* (1764), in which he supported the idea of a union of
all the British dominions on the basis of common commercial interests.

liberal tradition and defends her subjects, she also praises extravagantly someone like Pownall, with his etatist, imperialist, and pro-bureaucratic biases, as someone somehow particularly in tune with the "realities" of modern life. And there are hints that she would not disfavor the egalitarianism of some nineteenth-century followers. Generally, however, she keeps a high average, and there are not many other bad apples than the ones I have just named. And she is devoted enough to her subjects not to be taken in by Edmund Burke.

Another problem is that the book makes difficult reading; the style leaves much to be desired, and it assumes a considerable knowledge of eighteenth-century political history on the part of the reader, who would otherwise be lost in a sea of allusions. However, it remains an absolutely indispensable and highly valuable reference work for anyone interested in the history of libertarian thought or in the intellectual history of the eighteenth century. I would very strongly recommend it for National Book Foundation distribution.

Cordially,

Murray

6.

LETTER ON
WHAT IS POLITICAL PHILOSOPHY? BY LEO STRAUSS

January 23, 1960
Mr. Kenneth S. Templeton
William Volker Fund

Dear Ken:

The first thing to note about Leo Strauss's *What Is Political Philosophy?* is its surprising insubstantiality.[41] This is a rag-tag, hodgepodge of a book, consisting of bits and pieces of reviews, journal debates, etc. There is little of note in the book one way or another, and the book could only be of possible interest to someone who believes that every word Leo Strauss writes is worthy of immortality—a view I hardly share. Most of the book, indeed, consists of either book reviews by Strauss or answers to reviews of his books.

The book itself is, therefore, valueless and is only perhaps useful in gleaning Strauss's own political philosophy, about which bits and pieces come through to the reader. Fundamentally, I have always known, from Strauss's previous writings, that his work exhibits one great virtue and one great defect: the virtue is that he is in the forefront of the fight to restore and resurrect *political philosophy* from the interment given it by modern positivists and adherents of scientism—in short, that he wants to restore values and political ethics to the study of politics. This is surely a virtue indeed. The great defect is that Strauss, while favoring

---

[41]Leo Strauss, *What is Political Philosophy?* (Glencoe, Ill.: Free Press, 1959).

what he considers to be the classical and Christian concepts of natural law, is bitterly opposed to the seventeenth- and eighteenth-century conceptions of Locke and the rationalists, particularly to their "abstract," "deductive" championing of the natural rights of the individual: liberty, property, etc.

Strauss, in fact, has been the leading champion, along with Russell Kirk[42] and the Catholic scholars in America, of a recent trend in Locke historiography (e.g., in Peter Stanlis's book on *Edmund Burke and the Natural Law*[43]) to sunder completely the "bad," individualist natural-rights type natural law of the seventeenth and eighteenth centuries, from the "good" classical-Christian type—good, presumably, because it was so vague and so "prudential" that it offered very little chance to defend individual liberty against the state. In this reading, Hobbes and Locke are the great villains in the alleged perversion of natural law.

To my mind, this "perversion" was a healthy sharpening and development of the concept. My quarrel with Strauss, Kirk, et al., therefore, is not only valuational—that they are anti-natural rights and liberty, and I am for them—but also factual and historical: for they think that the Lockeans had an entirely different concept of natural law, whereas I think that the difference—while clearly there—was a sharpening

---

[42]Russell Kirk, an exponent of American conservatism, was editor of *Modern Age*, a journal published in Chicago by the Foundation for Foreign Affairs, founded in 1957. He is the author of *The Portable Conservative Reader* (New York: Penguin Books, 1982); *The Conservative Mind, from Burke to Santayana* (Chicago: Regnery, 1953); *Edmund Burke: A Genius Reconsidered* (Wilmington, Del.: Intercollegiate Studies Institute, 1997); *Prospects for Conservatives* (Washington, D.C.: Regnery Gateway, 1989); *Rights and Duties: Reflections on our Conservative Constitution* (Dallas: Spence Publications, 1997).

[43]Peter Stanlis, *Edmund Burke and the Natural Law* (Ann Arbor: University of Michigan Press, 1958). The author places Edmund Burke within the Thomist and late Scholastic tradition of natural law rather than in that of natural rights.

development, rather than a perversion or a diametric opposite. Take, for example, the Strauss-Kirkian overlook that while it is true that Aristotle and Plato were statists in their approach to natural law, the Stoics were fine individualists. I am glad to see that John Wild, in his *Plato's Modern Enemies and the Natural Law*,[44] agrees mainly with me, since he includes Tom Paine in his good natural-law galaxy—and no one is more anathema to the Strauss-Kirk types than Tom Paine.

Getting back to the book at hand, this defect and virtue are exhibited fully here, too. Strauss tilts lances at times against positivism, historicism, and scientism, and against modern democratic uniformity and conformity and its assault on privacy. He is opposed to the social-engineering amoralism of Machiavelli and to the pragmatism of Dewey. He even slaps down his leftish Thomist colleague Yves Simon for trying to maintain that Thomism implies democracy. But we also find more evidence of his concrete political position than was hitherto available, and much of it is disturbing.

We find Strauss backing nationalism and national tradition against cosmopolitans who prefer life and materialism; we find him praising "farsighted," "sober," British imperialism; we find him discoursing on the "good" Caesarism, on Caesarism as often necessary and not really tyranny, etc. He is suspicious, at least, of modern technology; in the fashion of Thomism, he persists in identifying society and the State (i.e., society with "political society"); he maintains that virtue is more important than freedom (the first cry of every statist); and he has the gall to talk about certain rulers not being tyrants because they were "legitimate," i.e., they were in the proper line of monarchic succession.

So far, Leo Strauss has all the stigmata of the Kirkian conservative at his worst; but the case is even worse than

---

[44]John Wild, *Plato's Modern Enemies and the Theory of Natural Law* (Chicago: University of Chicago Press, 1953).

this, for he includes in this an admixture of modern "progressivism": for he also believes that we don't really find the truth, the important thing being only to seek it (why bother seeking if it can never be found?), and he praises political philosophers for, yes, lying to their readers for the sake of the "social good"—i.e., to keep unpalatable truths from their readers because they believe that lies are necessary to the social fabric. I must say that this is an odd position for a supposed moralist to take. But then, this is one of the great weaknesses of the Kirkian-neo-Thomist approach to politics: its constant falling back upon the "prudential" as a great moral force, instead of an unfortunately necessary expediency of the moment. It is an approach that stems precisely from their refusal to be rationalist, "deductive," abstract, etc., in their approach to moral principle.

Intrinsically valueless as this book is, it has performed one service for me: the heavy downgrading of Leo Strauss in my estimation.

Cordially,

Murray

7.

LETTER ON
THOUGHTS ON MACHIAVELLI BY LEO STRAUSS

February 9, 1960
Dr. Ivan R. Bierly
National Book Foundation

Dear Ivan:

Leo Strauss's *Thoughts on Machiavelli* does not have, it is true, many of the weaknesses that I recently adumbrated in his *What is Political Philosophy?*, for it is *supposed* to be dealing with his one strong point: the adherence to political philosophy and ethics against modern, relativist "Machiavellianism."[45] Supposed to, I say, because this is the promise of his introduction, a promise that is really never fulfilled. And furthermore, while the book is not really strong on this one point of virtue, it exhibits other grave flaws in Strauss's thinking that only become evident in this particular book.

First, something should be said about the manner, the texture, the methodology of this book, which is really so absurd as to be almost incredible. It is based on the assumption, explicitly made at some points, that Machiavelli was a true Devil-figure, i.e., that he was evil, *and* that within this framework, he was all-wise, all-seeing, omniscient, etc. In short, a true Lucifer of titanic proportions. Taking his two books *The Prince* and *The Discourses* together, the result is that whenever Machiavelli contradicts himself in any way or omits something of note or puts in a particularly weak (to Strauss)

---

[45]Leo Strauss, *Thoughts on Machiavelli* (Glencoe, Ill.: Free Press, 1958).

argument or makes an error, Strauss immediately and persistently assumes that this simply *couldn't* be and that there must be some deep, twisted, hidden meaning to all this.

This is the Straussian method, and this is virtually the one method of textual analysis that he uses here. He had done similar things with Hobbes, Locke, etc., but not nearly so virulently. Now, it is true, as Strauss points out, that in those days, radical thinkers (i.e., thinkers against the usual stream) were wont to be circumspect, because they were in considerably more danger than they are today. But it is one thing to look for circumspection and quite another to construct a veritable architectonic of myth and conjecture based on the assumption of Machiavelli as an omniscient Devil, writing on a dozen different layers of "hidden meaning." The Straussian ratiocination is generally so absurd as to be a kind of scholar's version of the Great Pyramid crackpots or of the kind of screwball historians that flourish in the *American Mercury*. Strauss's methodology is to genuine history of political thought as astrology and numerology are to genuine astronomy.

If this seems extreme, I shall give a couple of examples of the almost excruciatingly crackpot nature of Strauss's scholarship (a crackpottiness that has to be discovered by rather careful reasoning, it is true, because of the density of the Straussian style.) These are two of innumerable examples.

First, Strauss's flight into numerology. On page 48, he remarks on what is to him the strange and wondrous fact that Machiavelli's *Discourses* have 142 chapters, the same number of chapters of Livy's *History*. To me, this is not at all surprising, since the *Discourses* are proclaimed to be a commentary on Livy's *History*. But this is enough for Strauss. This "strange fact" he says, "makes one wonder whether the number of chapters of the *Prince* is not also significant."[46] This somehow gives Strauss the clue that

---

[46]Ibid., p. 47.

there will be a linkage between the *Prince* and the 26th chapter of the *Discourses*. (Note the odd "reasoning": "Since the *Prince* consists of twenty-six chapters and the *Prince* does not give us any information as to the possible meaning of this number, we turn to the twenty-sixth chapter of the *Discourses*." Note the "since," as if this had the sweet logic of a syllogism.) Naturally, in this 26th chapter, Strauss finds mention of a "new prince," which sends him off on a lengthy flight of fancy—presented by him as scientific theory—where the true key to the *Prince* is found deep in the 26th chapter of the *Discourses*. On and on we go, until finally, on page 52, Strauss makes his crazy numerology explicit: "This is not the place to give further examples of Machiavelli's use of the number 26 or, more precisely, of 13 and multiples of 13. It is sufficient here to mention some further features of his work which would seem to indicate that numbers are an important device used by him."[47] And off we go further expecting at any moment to be introduced solemnly to the Mysteries of the Great Pyramid and the man-acle of Dr. Fu Manchu.

I grant that this is a particularly wild instance, but it is typical of the crackpot methodology that Strauss employs throughout. For example, in another place, Strauss says that Machiavelli, dedicating his *Prince* to Lorenzo de Medici, called upon him to "lead Italy to the promised land" by liberating her from barbarian rule and unifying her. To a sane reader, I submit, this is a complimentary call on Lorenzo to be another Moses. But to Strauss's odd mind, this is really a sly dig at Lorenzo, for after all Moses wasn't so great: he died before reaching the Promised Land. Therefore (*sic*), Machiavelli was *really* slyly deprecating Lorenzo as not good enough to reach the Promised Land, and subtly saying that only he, Machiavelli, was good enough. Another typical example of Strauss's nonsensical ratiocination.

---

[47]Ibid., p. 52.

The Straussian method alone, it seems to me, is enough to disqualify this book from National Book Foundation, or any other serious consideration, for that matter. Certainly if any book is a travesty on scholarship, this is it. But let us now push on from the method to the content of Strauss's ideas and his differences with Machiavelli, which aren't so good either. Now, it is true that Strauss criticizes Machiavelli for being amoral, pro-tyranny, interested only in social morality and the appearance of morality, etc. But the surprising thing to me was that there was really very *little* of this in the book, despite the promise of the introduction. For the main substance of the book is a bitter attack on Machiavelli, not for being unethical, but for being an atheist and a humanist. Strauss's bitter quarrel is largely theological, an attack on Machiavelli for being the first thinker to be non-Christian, to dismiss the Bible as fairy tales, etc.

Now, to paraphrase Max Eastman's classic review of Bill Buckley's *God and Man at Yale*, I do not believe that it should be the function of the National Book Foundation to lead American intellectuals to Jesus.[48] Surely, there are innumerable sources where anyone who wants to can imbibe Christianity without having special grants to disseminate it. This purely theological quarrel, with no ethical overtones except the complaint that Machiavelli substitutes interest in man for interest in God, takes up the bulk of Strauss's discourse on Machiavelli.

Finally, toward the end of the final chapter, Strauss leaves his favorite theme of *Christianity betrayed*, and turns to matters that concern us more: the ethical and the political. But even here, I found Strauss with as many or more bad points as good ones. For, he doesn't really *stress* Machiavelli being pro-tyranny, amoral, etc. What he stresses as much or more, are the following complaints against Machiavelli: he is pro-selfishness of the individual, as against the older concern for

---

[48]William F. Buckley, *God and Man at Yale: The Superstitions of Academic Freedom* (Chicago: Regnery, 1951).

the common good; he is pro-acquisitiveness, competition, material gain, and business activity, as against the older "virtues" of pure thought, leisure, etc.

Horror of horrors, in short, is that Machiavelli favors worldly gain, *worldly* comforts, the translation of thought into action in this world, as against mystical contemplation of God. The more I read Strauss's attack, the more I concluded that Machiavelli had more good points in his philosophy than I had imagined. Pushing this viewpoint to its logical conclusion, Strauss denounces the modern, Machiavellian emphasis on applying science to *this world* in the form of advancing technology. Technological inventions are apparently evil to Strauss and should be repressed by society (represented, of course, by the State). *This* is the final measure of Strauss's "conservatism."

Here are some quotations to give some of the flavor of the Straussian position as he concluded his book. Contrasting (good) classical philosophy to (bad) modern philosophy as ushered in by Machiavelli:

In classical philosophy, "the superiority of peace to war or of leisure to business is a reflection of the superiority of thinking to doing or making."[49]

Wicked Machiavelli

> achieves the decisive turn toward that notion of philosophy according to which its purpose is to relieve man's estate or to increase man's power or to guide man toward the rational society, the bond and the end of which is enlightened self-interest or the comfortable self-preservation of each of its members.[50]

(Once again: must Strauss push me into being a "Machiavellian"?)

---

[49]Strauss, *Thoughts on Machiavelli*, p. 295.

[50]Ibid., p. 296.

And finally, on the menace of inventions, here is how Strauss, in his concluding paragraph, describes the views of his obvious heroes, the "classical" philosophers:

> The classics were for almost all practical purposes what now are called conservatives. In contradistinction to many present day conservatives however, they knew that one cannot be distrustful of political or social change without being distrustful of technological change. Therefore they did not favor the encouragement of inventions. . . . They demanded the strict moral-political supervision of inventions; the good and wise city will determine which inventions are to be made use of and which are to be suppressed.[51]

(Lest you think he is referring to inventions for *war*, the fact is just the opposite; his heroes were forced by external conditions to encourage *only* inventions for war!)

All in all, then, I think it fair to say that Strauss's *Thoughts on Machiavelli* is bad in content or ideological position; it is certainly an execrable piece of scholarship. It deserves a very strong recommendation against use in the National Book Foundation program.

Cordially,

Murray

---

[51]Ibid., p. 298.

8.

LETTER ON
ON TYRANNY BY LEO STRAUSS

July 4, 1960
Dr. Ivan R. Bierly
William Volker Fund

Dear Ivan:

In Leo Strauss's *On Tyranny*, the author pursues the same sort of historical method in discussing political thought of the past that he later continued in his *Thoughts on Machiavelli*, i.e., the tortuous—and tortured—misreading of an author's work.[52] Strauss's specialty is the brusque rejection of the work, to search for—and quickly find—all manner of "hidden meanings" that diametrically contradict much of the actual text, and are based on unwarranted biases with which Strauss approaches the book. It must be emphasized that these "hidden meanings" are not "found" by searching the historical context in which the author wrote; Strauss is frankly a purely textual critic who is concerned with the text itself rather than the historical, or archaeological, setting.

On Tyranny is an analysis of the dialogue *Hiero*, written by the Greek philosopher Xenophon. In the dialogue, Hiero first tells the wise, visiting Greek Simonides that tyranny (Hiero is a tyrant) is a terrible thing, and then Simonides patiently explains to Hiero that only bad tyranny is wicked; that "good" tyranny, motivated by concern for the general

---

[52]Leo Strauss, *On Tyranny: An Interpretation of Xenophon's "Hiero"* (New York: Political Science Classics, 1948).

welfare, is really good, and should bring happiness to the tyrant. Hiero is apparently convinced.

Now, this is certainly a straightforward enough dialogue, consistent with the general position of the Greek philosophers, who—in contrast to their many virtues—always tended to assume that the State is the best instrument for achieving human goodness. Strauss, however, doesn't *like* this clear interpretation, and tries to spin an apologia for Xenophon by labored, and even absurd attempts to try to show that tyranny wasn't *really* defended, that Simonides was just trying to comfort his host, etc. Simonides was just wisely trying to work with given systems (e.g., tyranny) and trying to improve them—which, if true, I don't think says very much for the political philosophy of Simonides or his author, Xenophon—or, for that matter, of Strauss.

It is impossible to detail here the flights of fancy of the Straussian method, the unsupported assumptions of strategies, games, rhetorical victories and traps, etc., that he claims the two men engaged in to support his odd thesis—and with none of these assumptions really backed by solid evidence. I can only conclude that the book itself is worth little or nothing, and that Strauss himself is at his weakest when dealing in historical discussions of past political thinkers.

I can only conclude, once again, from my readings of Strauss, that Strauss is at his best on only one fundamental point: when he is criticizing ethical relativism and advocating a grounding of ethics on natural law (as he did in his relativism paper). Any more specific topics, however, either in detailed *content* of the natural law or in historical discussions of political philosophers, shows Strauss to be a fallacious political philosopher and a worse historian.

Cordially,

Murray

9.

THE SYMPOSIUM ON RELATIVISM: A CRITIQUE

Prefatory Note

Before embarking on a critique of the various papers on relativism, I think it important to delineate briefly what relativism is and what the issues are on this important topic. Let us first consider the polar opposite of relativism: absolutism. The absolutist believes that man's mind, employing reason (which according to some absolutists is divinely inspired, according to others is given by nature), is capable of discovering and knowing truth: including the truth about reality, and the truth about what is best for man and best for himself as an individual.

The relativist denies this, denies that man's reason is capable of knowing truth, and does so by claiming that rather than being absolute, truth is relative to something else. This something else may be different things, and so there can be many kinds of relativist; some of these things have been the subject of psychology of each individual, the economic interests of the individual (or of the "class" to which he belongs), the "Spirit of the Age" in which the person happens to live, the social structure of the society in which he lives, his "culture," his race, etc. Philosophically, I believe that libertarianism—and the wider creed of sound individualism of which libertarianism is a part—must rest on absolutism and deny relativism.

With these distinctions and definitions in mind, let us turn to the individual essays of the symposium.[53]

---

[53]The proceedings of the Symposium on Relativism were edited by Helmut Schoeck and James W. Wiggins and published in 1961 under the title *Relativism and the Study of Man* (Princeton, N.J.: D. Van Nostrand).

Bruno Leoni
"Some Reflections on the 'Relativistic' Meaning of the *Wertfreiheit* in the Study of Man"[54]

Paradoxically, this is a good paper even though I believe it fails in its ultimate purpose. For it is a good defense of Max Weber and his doctrine of *Wertfreiheit*. And in the course of this defense, Leoni shows that Weber did not attack scholars for having values or for advocating them, and that he was largely concerned, in his famous championing of a clear separation between fact and value, to be "confusion free," so that both the writer and the reader know what is going on. It was to Weber's eternal credit to point out that there is a place for value-free "social science" and for value-free analyses of the consequences of different policies, of different values even, without confusing matters by injecting the scholar's own false judgments into that discussion. And Leoni does well in stressing this contribution, and in joining Weber in attacking those social scientists who, pretending to *Wertfreiheit*, smuggle unanalyzed ethical preconceptions into their *wertfrei* analyses, and thus give the former the strictly scientific tone of the latter (e.g., those economists who naturally assume that "equality" or "stability" or "full employment" are good things and require certain policies, without bothering even to point out that they are slipping in a personal, unanalyzed value judgment.)

When all this is said and conceded, however, I must add that, in the famous battle at this symposium between Leoni and Mises on the one side and Strauss on the other, Leoni and Mises are wrong and Strauss is right. (And this is true even though Leoni corrects some Straussian errors about Weber: e.g., that Weber couldn't by his own doctrine make

---

[54]Bruno Leoni, "Some Reflections on the 'Relativistic' Meaning of the Wertfreiheit in the Study of Man," in Schoeck and Wiggins, eds., *Relativism*, pp. 158–74.

any selections or make any judgments *about* values—as Leoni indicates, and Mises shows elsewhere, making judgments of relevance or about values does *not* imply a value judgment on the part of the scholar.) For, in the final analysis, Leoni has to concede that ultimate ends—ultimate ethical values—are arbitrary and personal, and in fact, in an explicitly antirational section, he is scornful of the very idea that ethical values *should* be rationally demonstrated. To say, as Leoni does, that "if we need to 'demonstrate' the validity of our values to ourselves, this possibly means that we actually do not believe them enough to give up that 'demonstration' . . . if we try to demonstrate our values to other people, this is by no means the surest way of convincing them to accept those values," is sheer antirational obscurantism.[55] Values should be demonstrated because reason is the only sure, solid ground of conviction about values—far more solid than the emotional whims upon which Leoni would apparently base them. Strauss is right that the Weber position *is*, in the end, ethical relativism, because it holds that ethics are purely subjective and arbitrary, and not subject to rational demonstration; Strauss is right because he believes in the possibility and demonstrability of rational, objective ethics.

Leoni is also on shakier ground than Mises, because Mises's main discussion is on keeping economics and praxeology apart from ethics—which is a perfectly sound position—whereas Leoni is trying to keep ethics out of "political science." Now, while economics is a self-subsistent, *wertfrei* science, "political science" is not; modern political science is an empty, pretentious, quasi-mathematical set of "model building," and when we peel away the pretension, we find that "political science" is divisible into two parts: current *history* of political institutions or political thought, and political *philosophy*. And the very essence of political philosophy is the carving out of an ethical system—strictly, a subset of ethics dealing with political ethics. Ethics is the

---

[55]Ibid., p. 163.

one rational discipline that demands the establishment of a rational set of value judgments; political ethics is that subset applying to matters of State. Mises and Leoni both deny the existence of a rational, objective ethics; but Mises is at least left with praxeology and economics and valid sciences; Leoni is left with very little of "political science."

Another point that might confuse the readers: Leoni wrongly claims that the Weber position is one of "ethical absolutism" but "epistemological relativism." Mises, on the other hand, correctly describes their general position as one of "ethical relativism" and "epistemological absolutism."

Despite what I consider the ultimate failure of this paper, it is a good presentation of the Weber side of the dispute, and rehabilitates Weber from many superficial or excessive criticisms.

Ludwig von Mises, "Epistemological Relativism in the Sciences of Human Action"[56]

The bulk of this essay by Mises, the preeminent economist and praxeologist of our time, deals in his profound and unique way with a defense of economics against such relativist opponents as the historicists, who claimed that economic laws must be relative to each historical epoch. There are many excellent points made: an exposition of the Windelband-Rickert[57] refutation of positivist methods in the

---

[56]Ludwig von Mises, "Epistemological Relativism in the Sciences of Human Action," in Schoeck and Wiggins, eds., *Relativism*, pp. 117–34.

[57]Wilhelm Windelband (1848–1915) and Heinrich Rickert (1863–1936) were the most prestigious representatives of the School of Baden. Exponents of neo-Kantianism, they saw philosophy as a theory of values. The task of the philosopher was to establish which were the values at the base of knowledge, morality, and art. Another important contribution of Windelband and Rikert was their reflections on the foundation of history as a science.

sciences of human action; a critique of the deficiencies of the classical economists in confining themselves to a study of wealth and production, and therefore in fragmenting action into the "economic" and "noneconomic" spheres; critiques of the radical empiricists such as the intuitionalists, of Max Weber, and of the nature of historical events. In short, Mises attacks the various schools of epistemological relativism in the sciences of human action, and defends the absolute and eternal truths arrived at by the science of praxeology. As a result, this paper, as is almost any by Mises, is excellent and worth reading by every scholar. (I would consider the fundamental axioms of praxeology as based empirically on the nature of man rather than on "the logical structure of the human mind" as Mises does, but this is not important here.)

Having said this, and never being able to express how much of an enormous intellectual debt I owe to Mises, I must record two important defects in the paper, which stem from what I consider basic weaknesses in the Mises worldview. One is Mises's attempt to deny anyone the use of the concept "irrational." Mises categorically denies that anyone can ever act irrationally, either in the means he undertakes or in the ends for which he strives. I think this is flatly wrong, especially since Mises wishes to retain the concept of rational and apply it to all of man's actions. I cannot see how we can retain the term rational while denying anyone the use of its opposite: "irrational." If Mises maintains that no one can ever act irrationally, then he is simply using "rational" as a synonym for "purposive," and this means that he is using the term rational in a sense that no one else uses and is therefore illegitimate. Instead of denying that anyone could act irrationally, Mises should simply not use rational or irrational at all, and leave the term to psychology and ethics.

Thus, Mises asserts that we cannot say that the tribe using medicine men or a person in the Middle Ages using magic to attain their ends was irrational; after all, says Mises, they believed that their means were helping them to attain their ends (say, rainmaking or cure of disease), and a hundred years from now a doctor could just as well say that present-day doctors are "irrational" for using such a quaint method of cure as penicillin. The belief of the people using magic, however, is irrelevant to the issues; nobody denies that they thought they were accomplishing something.

Furthermore, magic is not in the same category as penicillin; for the use of penicillin rests on a scientific method, on an epistemology that can discover, by reason and by sense experimentation analyzed by reason, that penicillin can be used as a cure for disease. The fact that, fifty years from now, the advance of science will discover better cures does not make the present use of penicillin irrational—although, by the way, it would make the use of penicillin a hundred years from now irrational. But magic is in a completely different category; magic, by its very methodology is totally irrational and incapable of arriving at what it is supposed to achieve; and we can be assured that no "advance" a hundred years from now in the ritual of magic could ever improve its performance. The use of magic is therefore irrational, whether in the past, present, or future.

Moreover, not only can we say with absolute assurance that certain methods and means are irrational, but we can also go on to say that certain ends are irrational. Suppose that A's end is to torture B, because A enjoys it. Even if it lies within A's power to do so, and even if A need not fear retaliation by the police or by B or B's friends, I think it can be demonstrated that such torture and love of torture is contrary to the nature of man and to what is required by that nature for man's true happiness; I think it can be demonstrated that such perversions of man's nature are profoundly irrational. Yet Mises would insist on adding "from my personal point of view." It is not just my or your subjective "point of view" that decrees this; it is our objective, absolute insight into the discoverable nature of man.

What has happened here, and elsewhere, is that Mises has strayed off his great stomping ground, praxeology, on to a field, ethics, where he is, I believe, tragically wrong. For

irrationality or rationality of ends involves an ethical judgment, and Mises's subjectivity that we have just noted means
simply this: that Mises, while a praxeological or epistemological absolutist, is, unfortunately, an ethical relativist. To
Mises, there is no such a thing as absolute ethics; man, by
the use of his mind, cannot discover a true, "scientific"
ethics by insight into what is best for man's nature. Ultimate
ends, values, ethics, are simply subjective, personal, and
purely arbitrary. If they are arbitrary, Mises never explains
where they come from, how any individual arrives at them.
I can't see how he could arrive at any answer except the subjective, relative emotions of each individual.

This, Mises's ethical relativism, is his second great defect
in this paper, and we have seen how it is intimately tied up
with the first. As a result, Mises, excellent when he criticizes governments for opposing economics because economic science shows that governments cannot accomplish
their objectives, falters when he tries to refute the ethical
contentions of the statists.

Thus, Mises says, in his final section, that the enemies of
economics and of capitalism blame private enterprise as
immoral and materialistic, and praise Soviet Russia as well
as equality of incomes as more ethical. What can Mises
reply to this? Only that it is all "emotional talk," that praxeology and economics are neutral to ethics (true, but irrelevant), and that these statists should try to refute economic
teachings by "discursive reasoning, not by . . . appeal to arbitrary allegedly ethical standards."[58]

---

[58]Mises writes, "He who disagrees with the teachings of economics ought to try to refute them by discursive reasoning, not by
abuse, insinuations, and the appeal to arbitrary, allegedly ethical
standards." ("Epistemological Relativism in the Sciences of Human
Action," in *Money, Method, and the Market Process* (Auburn, Ala.:
Ludwig von Mises Institute, 1990), p. 51. First appeared in *Relativism and the Study of Man*, Helmut Schoeck and James W. Wiggins, eds. (Princeton, N.J.: D. Van Nostrand, 1962).

We can surely agree that it is illegitimate for anyone, leftist or libertarian, to ignore and not fully consider the value-free laws of economics. But precisely because economics is neutral to ethics, this is hardly an answer. For to Mises, all ethics is "arbitrary," and yet, even Mises must admit that no one can decide any policy unless he does make an ethical judgment. The man who understands economics and then chooses liberty is, or should be, considered by Mises to be just as "arbitrary" as the man who chooses egalitarianism, after accepting, say, the economic consequences of lessened productivity. And since either decision, according to Mises, is ultimately arbitrary, he cannot finally refute the interventionists in this way. And as for the opposition being "emotional," this may well be, but we have seen that emotion is the only groundwork that Mises can find for ultimate values anyway.

How has Mises been able to be an ethical relativist and still be the great champion that he has been of economic liberty? By what I consider an illegitimate assumption. Thus:

> Economics pointed out that many cherished (interventionist) policies . . . bring about . . . effects which—from the point of view of those who advocated and applied them—were even more unsatisfactory than the conditions which they were designed to alter.[59]

It is this assumption—that even the advocates really are worse off—that permits Mises to say that they are "bad." But how can Mises know what motivates the statists? Suppose, for example, the price controller wants power and doesn't care if it creates shortages; he has power and the perquisites of a soft job in the bureaucracy; suppose that he is a Communist, and wants to create shortages (or is a nihilist and hates everyone, and wants to create shortages); suppose that someone who wants to confiscate from the rich

---

[59]Mises, "Epistemological Relativism," p. 119.

has a very high time preference and doesn't care if the economy will be wrecked in twenty years. What then?

In short, it is illegitimate for Mises to assume that, knowing all the consequences shown by economics, everyone will consider himself worse off from the statist measure. When Mises says that repeal of such measures "would benefit the rightly understood or long-run interests of all the people," and are championed by vested "short-run interests," suppose, as we have just indicated, the time preferences of the latter are high; or suppose, even aside from the time preference, that the amount X can mulct from everyone by some interventionist measure is greater than the amount he will lose as a consumer.[60]

What I have been trying to say is that Mises's utilitarian, relativist approach to ethics is not nearly enough to establish a full case for liberty. It must be supplemented by an absolutist ethics—an ethics of liberty, as well as of other values needed for the health and development of the individual—grounded on natural law, i.e., discovery of the laws of man's nature. Failure to recognize this is the greatest flaw in Mises's philosophical worldview.

In his final section, Mises says that "there are authors who combine praxeological relativism with ethical relativism. But there are also authors who display ethical absolutism while rejecting the concept of universally valid praxeological laws."[61] Yes, and there is also a third category of writers: those who accept both praxeological and ethical absolutism, and recognize that both are vitally necessary for a complete philosophical view, as well as for the achievement of liberty.

I hope it is clear that this extended discussion is not intended to deny the great overall merits of Mises's paper and its importance for all scholars of human action.

---

[60]Ibid.

[61]Ibid.

Leo Strauss, "Relativism"[62]

I should make clear why I, a vehement critic of the books of Strauss's that I have read, consider this paper to be an excellent one. Strauss has one good point, and one alone: that there exists an absolute ethics for man, discoverable by reason, in accordance with the natural law of human nature. This is his good point, even though whenever he discusses the *content* of the ethics that he upholds, he becomes poor and questionable. But it is precisely this one good point to which he devotes his entire paper on relativism.

I have said in discussing Leoni's paper, that Strauss is right, and Mises and Leoni are wrong, and I say this even though in the *content* of their political positions, I am enormously more in agreement with Mises than with Strauss. Strauss's paper is devoted to a critique of ethical relativism (upheld by Mises, and particularly Leoni), and an argument on behalf of the existence of an objective, rational ethics.

The paper is rather oddly organized, being a series of criticisms of various relativists. Strauss begins with the almost incredibly confused and overrated Isaiah Berlin, and has no trouble demolishing Berlin and exposing his confusions—Berlin trying to be at the same time an exponent of "positive freedom," "negative freedom," absolutism, and relativism. He then proceeds to a very keen critique of the relativism of the famous Arnold Brecht.[63] Strauss shows, for

---

[62]Leo Strauss, "Relativism," in Schoeck and Wiggins, eds., *Relativism*, pp. 135–57.

[63]Arnold Brecht (1884–1977) was a civil servant in Germany. Under the Nazi regime he was arrested in 1933 and then released, after which he escaped to the United States. He began his academic career in the field of political science at the New School for Social Research in New York, where he remained until 1953, when he retired. At the center of Brecht's work was the development of political studies as a scientific discipline. He was the author of *Political Theory: The Foundations of Twentieth-Century Political Thought* (Princeton, N.J.: Princeton University Press, 1959), in which he

example, that in denying the possibility of rational ends, rational means are on not a very secure basis either:

> Reason [according to Brecht and the relativists] cannot even tell us that we ought to choose attainable ends; if someone "loves him who desires the impossible," reason may tell him that he acts irrationally but it cannot tell him that he ought to act rationally or that acting irrationally is acting badly or basely.[64]

From Brecht, Strauss proceeds to a fine critique of the positivist destruction of the principle of causality, a principle that is essential to rational absolutism. Strauss concludes here that "positivistic science in general and therefore positivistic social science in particular is characterized by the abandonment of reason or the flight from reason."[65]

Strauss then goes on to an interesting critique of the Marxist theoretician Georg Lukacs, showing that Lukacs, trying to escape from relativism, winds up as a relativist (Marxist-historicist variety) anyway. He also has some keen words of criticism about the Marxist vision of the change from "necessity" to "freedom" in the ultimate communist utopia.

After finishing with Lukacs, Strauss returns to logical positivism with a blistering critique of the weaknesses of positivism as a pure analysis of science, and an interesting

---

maintained, among other things, that values and ultimate aims could not be defined scientifically. He also wrote various works on themes relating to the institutional and constitutional problems of federalism and totalitarianism. Among others, see *Prelude to Silence: The End of the German Republic* (New York and London: Oxford University Press, 1944), *Federalism and Regionalism in Germany* (New York and London: Oxford University Press, 1945), and *The Political Education of Arnold Brecht: An Autobiography, 1884–1970* (Princeton, N.J.: Princeton University Press, 1970).

[64]Strauss, "Relativism," p. 144.

[65]Ibid. p. 145.

comparison of the positivists with their grandfather Hume, to the detriment of the former. Finally, Strauss delivers a very interesting and good critique of the "pessimistic" relativism of the existentialists.

I know that there were some emotional disagreements between Mises, Leoni, and Strauss at the symposium, but despite the fact that my personal sympathies are with the former, I must conclude that this is a very fine paper by Strauss, making many excellent points, and on the one topic where he can do a good job.

Eliseo Vivas, "Reiterations and Second Thoughts on Cultural Relativism"[66]

This is a fine paper, making some very keen criticisms of the cultural relativism engaged in by fashionable cultural anthropology, as well as a philosophic attack on cultural determinism: the idea that one's culture necessarily determines one's values. This concept is linked with cultural relativism, and receives a fine flailing from Vivas.

Vivas maintains that civilization is better, morally superior, to the cultures of primitive tribes, and bases his views on the position that knowledge of the nature of man permit one to say this. There are many sub-arguments, and all are worth reading. Adding to the merit of the article is Vivas's lucid style, which graces most of his writings.

While a gracefully stylistic paper, it is also a scholarly one, and Vivas provides reference leads to many recent works that appear to be promising: e.g., McGilvary, Macbeath, etc. There are also many pithy comments in passing about how the ancient Greeks knew all about the "cultural relativism" of numerous barbarian cultures, of how professional relativism has been used to weaken sexual

---

[66]Eliseo Vivas, "Reiterations and Second Thoughts on Cultural Relativism," in Schoeck and Wiggins, eds., *Relativism*, pp. 45–73.

morals, and entertaining bits of humor that highlight Vivas's points. And yet the logic is keen and clear, and we have such expositions as the paradoxes of relativism, and many other subtle arguments. And there is a refutation of the common idea that "relative" means "according to certain specific methods," which really serves as a refutation of Casserley's confusion of relativism with existing in actual space and time.[67]

The chief defect of Vivas's paper, which does not, however, offset the many merits of the piece, is Vivas's agnosticism about what ethics we really *do* know. He upholds the *possibility* of an objective, rationally arrivable ethics, but when it comes to specific content, he virtually denies that such ethics have been found yet (aside from a very few generalities such as: civilization is better than savagery, and Ilse Koch was bad). His belief that almost all objective knowledge lies ahead of us weakens his ultimate position against the relativists; it is surely an entirely unnecessary view. Several thousand years of life among men, and of perfection upon it, have built up a pretty rigorous, and extensive body of objective knowledge of the nature of man, and what is best for him. Of course, it can and should be added to, and the more specific sciences such as economics or biology or psychology are developed, the more it is added to, but the basic structure and contents remain, and these contents are very broad.

In the whole, however, Vivas's paper is very worthwhile, and a fine contribution to the symposium.

---

[67]Julian Victor Langmead Casserley (1909–1978), was professor of theological philosophy, author of *Morals and Man in the Social Sciences* (London, New York: Longmans, Green, 1951), *The Christian in Philosophy* (New York: Scribner, 1951), *Graceful Reason: The Contribution of Reason to Theology* (Greenwich, Conn.: Seabury Press, 1954), *Retreat from Christianity in the Modern World* (London: Longmans, Green, 1952), and *Toward a Theology of History* (New York: Holt, Rinehart and Winston, 1965). Casserley was one of the participants of this symposium.

Leonard Carmichael,
"Absolutes, Relativism, and the Scientific Psychology
of Human Nature"[68]

I am extremely impressed with Mr. Carmichael's paper. This is a highly important and pioneering effort to ground a set of natural-law ethics and values on the biological nature of man and what is best for man. I think one of the most important directions to be pursued in the "sciences of human action" is to develop a natural-law ethics based on nature rather than, or at least to supplement, ethics based on theological revelation. Carmichael is here undertaking this from his vantage point as a biologist. This provides a truly absolutist, and yet "scientific," grounding for ethics.

Carmichael begins, in happy omen, by resurrecting Herbert Spencer, and showing that Spencer must be modified to eliminate his bias for an *evolutionary* ethics, since man has already fully "evolved," since he has not physically changed in all historic time. Carmichael then goes on to look for those stable absolutes in human nature that could be used to base an absolute ethic. First, Carmichael shows that biological organisms tend to remain with constant qualities—biological "conservatism."[69] While human individuals are variable *within* each generation, the average man doesn't change basically from one century to the next. (The tools built by Bronze Age men would fit the men of today, etc.) Carmichael goes on to point, keenly, to such other human psychological and physiological constants as symmetry (e.g., cave drawings), rhythm, texture, perception through human sense organs, etc. From this, Carmichael hints brilliantly at the derivation of an absolute natural law esthetics. Thus

---

[68]Leonard Carmichael, "Absolutes, Relativism, and the Scientific Psychology of Human Nature," in Schoeck and Wiggins, eds., *Relativism*, pp. 1–22.

[69]Ibid., p. 4.

the great arts, such as architecture, sculpture, painting, music, and the dance, are built upon these fixed relationships between the unchanging character of the physics of radiant energy (light) and of material vibrations (sound) and the organism. Hence each art acquires its canons that determine the relationships which are and which are not evaluated as good or bad by human sight and hearing. Once such values are established, only a changing romantic whimsy or caprice can pretend that they are not fixed and immutable so long as human brains comprehend and senses remain fixed.[70]

I am enthused over this type of approach because I believe that work along such paths could bear a great deal of fruit in working out a viable system of absolute ethics, esthetics, and values in general.

The fact that an eighteenth-century nobleman and a primitive Indian had different table manners, avers Carmichael, does not prove relativism, for the important point is that both the nobleman and the savage needed and ate food. There is variation, but there is also a nexus of fixed norms. Monogamy may be demonstrable as absolutely the best form of marriage for developing the emotional characteristics of the human personality and also for child rearing. Then, Carmichael goes on to criticize the "Gallup Poll" moralists for trying to prove that the very fact that some practices exist makes them moral or normal. He maintains that the civilized human race has, over the centuries, found ethical norms and practices that are absolutely better than others; but they must be inculcated in each generation of the young.

Carmichael also has good criticisms of the view that growing up in a New Guinea hut is just as good as going to Harvard, or that the latest nonobjective-art nonsense is as

---

[70]Ibid., pp. 6–7.

good as Titian. The latter alternatives are absolutely better. While friendly to religion, Carmichael also sees that the rational discovery of natural law is just as viable as the absolute alternative to relativism:

> The question as to whether a code of social living is *revealed* and established as fixed as a series of Divine Commandments given to men or *discovered* as absolutes of social law by human trial and error may turn out to be different ways of viewing the same set of rules. . . . Both the ideas of the revelation and of the discovery of social and esthetic values are opposed to the notion that all such concepts are merely relativistic and changeable and have no fixed sanction of any kind.

Very well put.

Applying this approach to law, Carmichael sees that new technology does not render legal principles obsolete. On the contrary, absolute and eternal legal principles are *applied* by judges to the problems of new technology.

The relativist, says Carmichael perceptively, is essentially a romantic who judges everything by his own subjective emotions and whimsy; for the romantic, all the rules of life are simply arbitrary, man-made conventions that he defies at the behest of his emotions. The absolutist, on the other hand, is a classicist, who discovers and then adheres to fixed truths, and is guided, presumably, by reason. Education, then, becomes vitally the inclination, the passing on, of these truths in the various fields of ethics, esthetics, etc. Literature of the past is valuable in discovering how the great men of the past dealt with eternally human problems and the rules that they arrived at.

Especially in the latter part of the paper, Carmichael shows an unfortunate tendency to accept various mystical rather than rational procedures for arriving at these fixed truths, but this hardly offsets what I consider to be the great value of this paper and the general approach that it embodies.

Final Comments

On the whole, I think this can be set down as another successful Volker Fund symposium. There were many first-rate papers, even if they were not always correct. Profound and basic controversies, such as those between Leoni and Mises against Strauss on relativism and relativist ethics, help rather than hurt the symposium as a whole, for the reader has a chance to read and weigh excellent presentations of both sides of this critical issue. Of the twelve papers, I consider six as first rate: those of Carmichael, Leoni, Mises, Pei, Strauss, and Vivas. . . .[71] Three could be considered fair, or moderately good: Casserley, Tietz, and Weaver. Only three I would rate as downright poor: Schoeck, Malin, and Zirkle, especially the latter two— Schoeck for his lengthy diatribe against individual liberty, Malin for his wallowing in a confused mysticism and his worship of primitive man, Zirkle for his extreme (and relativist) espousal of a social Darwinist, evolutionist ethic. I think this is a good record for an interdisciplinary gathering of such varied individuals from such diverse disciplines.

---

[71]For the purposes of this book, I have only included Rothbard's critiques for five of the articles that he considered first rate. The sixth is Mario Pei's "Relativism in Linguistics."

10.

ON POLANYI'S *THE GREAT TRANSFORMATION*

June, 1961
To: Robby
William Volker Fund

Karl Polanyi's *The Great Transformation* is a farrago of confusions, absurdities, fallacies, and distorted attacks on the free market.[72] The temptation is to engage in almost a line-by-line critique. I will abjure this to first set out some of the basic philosophic and economic flaws, before going into some of the detailed criticisms.

One basic philosophic flaw in Polanyi is a common defect of modern intellectuals—a defect that has been rampant since Rousseau and the Romantic Movement: *worship of the primitive*. At one point (in dealing with the Kaffirs[73]), Polanyi actually uses the maudlin phrase "noble savage," but

---

[72]Karl Polanyi, *The Great Transformation* (New York: Holt, Rinehart and Winston, 1944). Polanyi's *great transformation* was the degeneration into authoritarianism of the liberal institutions in the 1920s and '30s. He denied the liberal axiom according to which a market society was a natural historical outcome; he therefore tried to demonstrate the artificiality and the pathological nature of the liberal market, which could only end in a violent crisis. The processes leading to fascism refuted the economic theory of a market able to regulate itself, which, for Polanyi, was only a utopia. As a result, Polanyi criticized the classical economical school and the free market. In Polanyi's opinion, the free market could only produce a dangerous individualism and social disaggregation. Therefore "society," in order to defend itself, had to regulate the market by introducing control and redistributive mechanisms. Fascism and Communism were the historical proof of the impossibility of the self-regulating market.

[73]A South African tribe.

this idea permeates the book.[74] Modern Rousseauism
received a major impetus from the cultural anthropologists,
such as Ruth Benedict, Margaret Mead, Franz Boas, and the
like (many of whom were Communists, and the remainder
highly left-wing), who went eagerly to visit the existing primitive tribes, and reported back about the gay, happy life of
Tribe X which had no private property and no inhibitions
imposed by monogamous marriage.[75]

There are several things to be said about this worship of
the primitive. First, it is absolutely illegitimate to infer, as
Polanyi does, the history of pre-Western civilization *from*
analysis of *existing* primitive tribes. Let us never forget that
the existing primitive tribes are precisely the ones that *didn't*
progress—that remained in their primitive state. To infer
from observing them that this is the way our ancestors
behaved is nonsense—and apt to be the reverse of the truth,
for our ancestors presumably behaved in ways that quickly
advanced them *beyond* the primitive stage thousands of
years ago. To scoff, therefore, at the idea that our ancestors
among primitive tribes engaged in barter, and then in monetary exchange, etc., on the basis of the magic and games
indulged in by *present-day* primitives, is a blunder of the
highest order.

---

[74]Polanyi, *The Great Transformation*, p. 202. Rothbard notes,
"For an excellent discussion of Rousseau, primitivism and the
Romantic Movement, see Irving Babbit, *Rousseau and Romanticism*
(Boston and New York: Houghton Mifflin, 1935)."

[75]Ruth Benedict (1887–1948) was an American anthropologist
whose work had a strong influence in the field of cultural anthropology. She studied with Franz Boas at Columbia University, where
she later taught. After eleven years of study in the field among
Native Americans, she published *Tales of the Cochiti Indians* (1931)
and *Patterns of Culture* (1934), emphasizing how the attitudes of a
particular culture contributed deterministically to defining an individual's personality. In 1940, to combat Nazi racial theories, she
published *Race: Science and Politics*. She was recognized as one of
the most important anthropologists in the United States and was
president of the American Anthropological Association.

Second, it is implicitly and even explicitly assumed that the way primitive tribes act is more "natural," and somehow more appropriate to man than the "artifices" of civilization. This is at the root of Rousseauism. The way ignorant, fear-ridden, quasi-animalistic savages act is somehow more natural—because presumably more "instinctual"—than the ways of civilization. This is the root of Rousseau's, and many other leftists' view that man is "naturally good," but is corrupted by his institutions. This basic idea is fundamentally and radically *antihuman*, because it denies the basic facts about human nature and the way human beings must necessarily operate. Animals are born with "instincts"; these instincts are, in essence, sense-determined responses. Animals do not possess a free will or rational consciousness, hence they can only adapt, in sensory fashion, to their environment. Man, on the other hand, can *alter* his given environment by use of his reason and his free will.

Man is born a *tabula rasa*; he must learn how to choose the ends that are proper for him and the means that he must adopt to attain them. All this must be done by his reason.

Civilization is precisely the record by which man has used his reason to discover the natural laws on which his environment rests, and to use these laws to alter his environment so as to suit and advance his needs and desires. Therefore, worship of the primitive is necessarily corollary to, and

---

Margaret Mead (1901–1978), an American anthropologist, studied with Franz Boas and Ruth Benedict. Author of the famous *Coming of Age in Samoa* (1928), her numerous works also include *Growing up in New Guinea* (1930) and *Sex and Temperament in Three Primitive Societies* (1935). She worked at the American Museum of Natural History in New York.

Franz Boas (1858–1942), a German anthropologist, was founder of a school of anthropology based on the concept of cultural relativism. He spent a large part of his career at Columbia University in New York. He specialized in the culture of the Indians of North America and had numerous students who continued to develop cultural anthropology. Author of *The Mind of the Primitive Man* (1911), *Primitive Art* (1927), and *Language and Culture* (1940).

based upon, an attack on man's reason and intellect. It is this deep-seated "anti-intellectualism" that leads these people to proclaim that civilization is "opposed to nature" and that the primitive tribes are closer to it. It is this opposition to the mind and to reason that leads them to, for example, worship the Negro as being more "instinctual," "sexier," closer to nature, etc. And because man is supremely the "rational animal," as Aristotle put it, this worship of the primitive is a profoundly antihuman doctrine.

Antihuman, antirational doctrine, then, eagerly looks to illiterate, savage, fear-ridden primitives as people on whom we—the heirs of 2,000 years of the finest products of civilization and the human race—are supposed to model ourselves. If an existing primitive tribe has no private property or engages in indiscriminate promiscuity, this should be all the more reason for us to do the reverse.

The myth is then coined of the "happy savage," that these primitives are truly happy and content. This myth permeates the Polanyi volume. Let us shed the vestiges of romantic mythology and look at these savages as they are. They are, in the first place, complete slaves to their environment. When the fruit tree is in bloom, they can perhaps subsist by picking the fruit off the tree; but suppose there is a blight, one year, on fruit trees? What happens to this "happy-go-lucky" tribe? It dies, *en masse*. It is no wonder that the primitive tribes are all small in number.

Second, the primitive's life is a life of almost constant terror: terror of the world about him, which he does not and cannot understand, since he has not engaged in any sort of scientific, rational inquiry into its workings. We know what a thunderstorm is, and therefore do not fear it, and can take rational measures against lightning; the savage does not know, and therefore surmises that the god of the thunder is displeased with him, and that therefore that god must be propitiated with votive offerings and sacrifices (sometimes human sacrifices).

Since the savage has no concept of a world knit together by natural law (a concept that employs reason and science), he believes that the world is governed by a whole host of capricious spirits and demons, each of which can only be propitiated—with only partial "success"—by ritual, by magic, and by a priestcraft of witch doctors who specialize in this propitiation. So fearful is the savage that he can do nothing on his own, that his individuality is virtually completely undeveloped—because the individual savage makes almost no use of his reason and of his mind. Therefore, virtually everything the savage does is governed by immutable, utterly irrational, taboos or command: by custom.

And *this* is the fear-ridden, barely human, creature whom we, people who have used our intellect to "conquer" nature, are being asked to emulate, whom Polanyi extols as being truly "social," and as being happily free of the "inhuman" despotism of the free market!

Moreover, the life of the savage, as Hobbes put it, is "nasty, brutish, and short." His life expectancy is very short, and his life is ravaged by all manner of disease, disease that he can do nothing about except give food to witch doctors to utter incantations. The increasing conquest of disease has been made possible only by the advance of civilization: by the use of reason, by capitalism, and by the market.

Polanyi admires the tribal and other caste societies, because "nobody starves."[76] Everyone might admittedly be on a subsistence level, he concedes, but no individual starves. Is it that great a comfort that everyone starves together? This is a grotesque statement. The primitive world is—indeed all worlds before the Industrial Revolution were—constantly racked by famine and by plague. "Famine" was a continual occurrence before the Industrial Revolution; since the Industrial Revolution we have never heard of famine (the only recent famines have been in Communist China, and earlier, in Soviet Russia). Famine emerges from a lack of interlocal trade; when one locality's food crop fails,

---

[76]Polanyi, *The Great Transformation*, p. 210.

since there is virtually no trade with other localities, the bulk of the people starve. It is precisely the permeation of the free market throughout the world that has virtually ended this scourge of famine by permitting trade between areas. It is this market that Polanyi castigates as the bringer of virtually all evils.

Polanyi admires all societies of caste and status: tribal, mercantilist, or whatnot. A caste society, he maintains, provides "security." Famines and plagues: are they "security"? No amount of restrictionism can provide that *production* from which any economic "security" must come; in fact, just the opposite, for all caste restrictions, all restrictions on the market, simply cripple and hinder production, and thus keep everyone at or near subsistence level.

In fact, the Asiatic "extended family" system has kept China, Indonesia, etc., in primitive poverty and misery for centuries. This "share and share alike" custom, which Polanyi undoubtedly admires, decrees that as soon as any individual makes a little more money, he must distribute it *pro rata* among a whole host of distant, as well as near, relatives. As a result of this "noble" system, there is no incentive for any individual Chinaman to earn more and produce more and hence, the Chinese did not (before Communism) do so and did not progress. In Java, the village commune system—definitely Polanyiesque—means that a starving, massively overpopulated Java has been exploiting and tyrannizing the much more progressive and capitalistic islands of Indonesia (e.g., Sumatra).

The "security" of the caste system is the security of the prison house. (By the way, anyone who wants "security" in a market economy can always commit a crime and go to jail, where Polanyiesque security will be furnished to him.) This "security" means an all-pervasive *hopelessness* in a caste society. The son of a baker must always be a baker, even if his interests and abilities are completely elsewhere. No one can rise; no one can shift his occupation or do anything differently from his ancestors. This is the annihilation of all that is most vital, most purposeful, most *alive*, in the life of any individual.

Another basic flaw in any caste society—and ignored by Polanyi—is the problem of population growth. The witch doctor, the custom of tribe, the chief or king, and Professor Polanyi can all decree that X and the son of X be a baker, Y and the son of Y be a farmer, etc., but what happens when population increases, as it almost inevitably tends to do? What does the younger son do? Polanyi sneers at Malthus but the Malthusian problem is always supremely evident in the caste society. What happens when the "natural checks" of famine and disease do not work sufficiently?

This is why the caste-communal society of Sparta put their babies out in the woods for an "exposure test," not because the Spartans were inherently a cruel people but because they were faced with what was, in the context of their social structure, an insoluble problem: what to do with their population increase. It was population growth, further, that was wrecking mercantilist Europe. Population growth was the reason for the rise of able-bodied beggars and thieves in eighteenth-century England. There was no work for them to do. It was the rise of capitalism—the advance of capital to provide them with jobs, the expansion of the market to produce cheap goods for the masses—that not only enormously increased the standard of living of the masses but also provided jobs for these increasingly "excess" people.

Furthermore, Polanyi continues the old anti-capitalist canard that the Industrial Revolution was made possible by the enclosure movement, which supposedly drove sturdy yeomen off their lands and into the cities.[77] This is nonsense; not only did the enclosure movement enclose the "commons" and not people, and by the great increase in agricultural productivity provide the wherewithal in resources and

---

[77]In England in the eighteenth century, vast areas of the country were common land and were cultivated under the open field system. From 1830 on, the development of crop growing techniques made the large farms more efficient and almost all agricultural land was enclosed. According to Polanyi, this led to a mass exodus of small farmers from the countryside.

income for the Industrial Revolution, but also the enclosures did *not* drive people off the land. The surplus population in the rural areas was a consequence of *population growth*; it was this increase in rural population that drove these desperate people into the cities to look for work.

Capitalism did *not*, therefore, tragically disrupt, as Polanyi would have it, the warm, loving, "social" relations of pre-capitalist era. Capitalism took the outcasts of society— the beggars, the highwaymen, the rural overpopulated, the Irish immigrants—and gave them the jobs and wages that moved them from destitution to a far higher standard of living and of work.

It is easy enough to wring one's hands at the child labor in the new British factories; it is, apparently, even easier to forget what the child population of rural England was doing before the Industrial Revolution—and during the Industrial Revolution, in those numerous areas of England where it and the new capitalism had not yet penetrated: these children were dying like flies and living in infinitely more miserable conditions. *This* is why we read nowadays, when it seems inexplicable to us, British and American writings of the period that praise the new factories for giving work to women and children![78] This praise was not due to their being inhuman monsters; it was due to the fact that, before such labor was available (and in those regions where such labor was not available) the women and children were living and suffering in infinitely worse conditions. Women, children, immigrants, after

---

[78]Rothbard, it would seem, was referring to the story of Hannah More, mentioned by Polanyi, from Joseph Palmer's *The Lancashire Colliery Girl* (1795). In this story, the author praises a Lancashire girl who worked in a mine from the age of nine with her younger brother. Hannah More stressed the fact that the two children were very useful members of society, and that the girl's qualities were recognized by her employers (Hannah More, *Cheap Repository Tract*, described in Polanyi, *The Great Transformation*, p. 220). The story has an "edifying" ending because the girl manages to raise herself to a level of greater independence by finding work with a family as a servant.

all, were not driven to the factories with whips; they went voluntarily and gladly, and that is the reason.

There are even broader aspects of the population problem that Polanyi ignores. For capitalism was responsible, in a sense, for the huge increase in population in the modern world. Capitalism's upsurge in living standards has enabled capitalism to free the world from the Malthusian checks, from the grim evils of overpopulation, and has permitted a rapid multiplication of population at even higher living standards than before. So when Polanyi, in effect, asks us to scrap the market and return to a caste or communal or even tribal society, he is *not only* asking us to abandon the luxuries of civilization and return to the subsistence level of the primitive tribe; he is also asking for the liquidation and eradication of the vast bulk of the world's population, because, if a caste or tribal system will "work"—even on the least subsistence level—it will work only for a small, tiny minority of the population; the rest of us will starve *en masse*. The small numbers of the primitive tribe noted above, takes on, then, a new and more terrible significance.[79]

In all of his complaining about *laissez-faire* and the free market, Polanyi somehow overlooks probably the single most important aspect of this system: freedom. In a free society, *no one compels* Polanyi or anyone else to join in the free market. If Polanyi or any other critic is so hostile to the alleged tyranny, "instability," etc., of the market, the free society *leaves them free to get out*. Anyone, at any time, can leave the market: can go off in the woods and live on berries in a cave, can buy his own farm and be completely self-sufficient, cut off from the rest of the world, or can vary his participation as much as he likes. Anyone who wants to can, in a free society, even join a voluntary commune, like Brook Farm or an Israeli kibbutz, and lead as blissfully communistic a life as he or she

---

[79]Rothbard notes, "For a refutation of the enclosure myth and a recognition of the key being increase of population, see W.H.B. Court, *A Concise Economic History of Britain from 1750 to Recent Times* (Cambridge: Cambridge University Press, 1954)."

wishes. Since everyone still has the option to do so, since any-one has the option to go off to a desert island or join a com-mune, *why is Polanyi bitter about the market*??

In fact, the free society leaves everyone such options. Why, in that case, has the free *market* flourished when peo-ple have been left free—flourished until it brought about cap-italist civilization? The reason is precisely that the vast bulk of the people, in the past and in the present ages, don't agree with Polanyi: they vastly preferred the so-called instability, unhappiness, et al. of the market to the supposedly happy subsistence life of a communal savage! For if they had not vastly preferred it, they would not have joined the market; they would have sacrificed monetary income for their tribal or self-sufficient farm life. *Yet they did not.* There is no bet-ter way of thoroughly refuting Polanyi's weeping about the lost glories of "society" than to observe the numberless mil-lions who have chosen the way of the market when they had the free choice.

In fact, it is precisely such left-wing intellectuals as Polanyi who are always weeping about the "Coca-Colaiza-tion" of the rest of the world and bemoaning the supposedly lost glories of "folk culture" in the undeveloped countries. For as soon as they get the chance, peoples all over the world, regardless of cultural tradition, abandon their sup-posedly beloved culture in order to adopt Western ways, Western clothes, get a Western-type job or serve Western tourists, and earn Western money—and drink Coca-Cola and go to Hollywood movies, as well. It took only a few years, for example, for the people of Japan to abandon their thousand-year-old traditional culture and folkways to turn eagerly to these supposedly decadent market-brought goods of the West. Why is that? Is it Western "imperialism"? Are Amer-ican troops forcibly drugging everyone with Coca-Cola?[80]

---

[80]Rothbard notes, "For an inspiring and scholarly discussion of the enormous growth of a market and exchange economy among illit-erate natives of West Africa, I strongly recommend P.T. Bauer, *West African Trade* (Cambridge: Cambridge University Press, 1954)."

Even backward countries that are hostile to capitalism—such as India, Ghana, etc.—do not at all reject the fruits of Western civilization on behalf of their seemingly joyful tribal traditions. On the contrary, they want Western products and conveniences; it is just that they have not understood that capitalism is needed to obtain them.

Given a choice, then, almost everyone chooses the market economy and its advanced civilization, even, curiously enough, Professor Polanyi himself, who most conspicuously did *not* rush off to some tribe or commune.

Why, then, do we consider the free market as "natural," as Polanyi sneeringly asks? The reason is that the free market is (1) what men have turned to when they have been allowed freedom of choice, and (2) what men *should* turn to if they are to enjoy the full stature of men, if they are to satisfy their wants, and mold nature to their purposes. For it is the market that brings us the standard of living of civilization.

In his book, Polanyi is continually assuring us that his beloved primitive natives do nothing at all for personal "gain"; only for magic, for what he calls "reciprocity," etc. What is so bad about gain, which Polanyi virtually assumes to be a malevolent word? The principle of the free market is voluntary exchange for mutual benefit. This mutual benefit constitutes gain. The free market is, in fact, that interpersonal relationship which does insure mutual benefit by all relating parties. Why does Polanyi find this so obnoxious? Why, at every point, does he seem to prefer an interpersonal relation where only one party gains? For if only one party gains it follows that the other party loses; in short, it follows that for Polanyi, the ideal relationship between people is *not* mutual gain, but *exploitation*: the gain of one at the expense of another.

Is *this* the "moral," "social" relationship for which we are supposed to abandon market economy and civilization itself? Why is it that every socialist hates and contemns the exchange relationship—the supposedly "calculating," "inhuman" relationship where *both* parties gain? Do they consider it more moral for A to let himself be exploited by B, and for

B to exploit A? For make no mistake, when the socialist condemns A for not *giving* money to B without receiving anything—material or spiritual—in exchange, he is calling upon A to be a sacrificial animal for the benefit of an exploiting B.

In his discussion of his beloved primitive tribes, Professor Polanyi says that they deal with each other, not on the basis of (Ugh!) mutual gain, but on the basis of "reciprocity" and "redistribution."[81] The "principle of redistribution" is, of course, this same principle of *exploitation*. It is the "redistribution," coerced by the State or the tribe, from the producers to the parasitic class favored by the tribal or State chiefs.

As for the "principle of reciprocity," Polanyi is certainly unclear about just what it entails. To some small extent—to the extent that the process is rational—this is simply exchange or barter, smuggled in by the conceptual back door. To the extent it is not rational, it is either play or sport—which hardly needs further comment—or it is ritual magic, which has been commented on above. It is apparently the latter part of "reciprocity" that Polanyi extols, for he is apparently enchanted by the "Kula trade" in which one island gives certain objects to another island, and will only receive similar (or the same?) stuff back years or decades later from some other island in the ring.[82] What Polanyi

---

[81]Polanyi, *The Great Transformation*, p. 63.

[82]Ibid., p. 65. Kula trading is typical of the archipelago of the Trobriand Islands, a group of islands arranged in the form of a circle in western Melanesia. Polanyi describes their form of trading:

> Still, it is trade, and large expeditions are undertaken periodically by natives of this approximately ring-shaped archipelago in order to carry one kind of valuable object to peoples living on distant islands situated clockwise, while other expeditions are arranged carrying another kind of valuable object to the islands of the archipelago lying counterclockwise. In the long run, both sets of objects . . . will move round the archipelago, a traject which may take them up to ten years to complete. (p. 66)

especially likes about this is its lack of true mutual gain—or is it its obvious pointlessness? And, again, *must* we follow the path of a magic-ridden group of savages?

I mentioned that the free society would permit Polanyi or any who agree with him to abandon the market and find whatever other forms suit them. But one thing and *one thing* alone the free society would *not* permit Polanyi to do: to use coercion over the rest of us. It will let him join a commune, but it will *not* let him force you or me into his commune. This is the sole difference, and I therefore must conclude that *this* is Polanyi's sole basic complaint against the free society and the free market: they do not permit him, or any of his friends, or anyone else, to use force to coerce someone else into doing what Polanyi or anyone else wants; they do not permit force and violence; they do not permit dictation; they do not permit theft; they do not permit exploitation. I must conclude that the type of world that Polanyi would force us back into, is precisely the world of coercion, dictation, and exploitation.[83] And all this in the name of "humanity"? Truly, Polanyi, like his fellow thinkers, is the "humanitarian with the guillotine."[84]

The naked and open advocacy of force and exploitation would, of course, not get very far; and so Polanyi falls back on the fallacy of methodological holism, treating "society" as a real entity in itself, apart from and above the existence or interests of the individual members. The market, Polanyi thunders, disrupted and sundered "society";[85] restrictions on the market are "society's" indispensable

---

[83]Rothbard notes, "Unfortunately, historically, most of humanity has lived and suffered, up until the advent of the free market. See K. Wittfogel, *Oriental Despotism* (New Haven, Conn.: Yale University Press, 1957)."

[84]Rothbard notes, "See Isabel Paterson's profound work of political theory, *The God of the Machine* (New York: G.P. Putnam's Sons, 1943)."

[85]Polanyi, *The Great Transformation*, p. 310.

method of "protecting itself."[86] All very well, until we begin to inquire, *who is* "society"? Where is it? What are its identifiable attributes?

Whenever someone begins to talk about "society" or "society's" interest coming before "mere individuals and their interest," a good operative rule is this: guard your pocketbook. And guard yourself! Because behind the facade of "society," there is always a group of power-hungry doctrinaires and exploiters, ready to take your money and to order your actions and your life. For, somehow, they "are" society!

The only intelligible way of defining society is as the array of voluntary interpersonal relations. And preeminent among such voluntary interrelations is the free market! In short, the market (and the interrelations arising from the market) is society, or at least the bulk and the heart of it. In fact, contrary to the statements by Polanyi and others that sociability and fellowship come before the market, the truth is virtually the reverse; for it is only because the market and its division of labor permit mutual gain among men that they can *afford* to be sociable and friendly, and that amicable relations can ensue. For in the jungle, in the tribal and caste societies, there is not mutual benefit but *warfare* for scarce resources!

Curiously, in his idyllic picture of tribal life, Polanyi never seems to mention pervasive intertribal warfare. Such warfare is almost necessary because groups of people are fighting over scarce resources: water holes, hunting, etc.

Tribalism, not capitalism, is the "rule of the jungle," for warfare and extermination of the "unfit" is the only way that some of the tribes can keep alive. It is the capitalist market economy which *increases* resources by mutual benefit, that is able to bypass the rule of the jungle and to rise above such

---

[86]The second part of Part 2 of Polanyi's volume was entitled "Self-Protection of Society." Cf. Polanyi, *The Great Transformation* pp. 167–280. He deals with the movements that tried to limit the market, Owenism, Chartism, unionism, and other social-protection movements of various types.

animal-like existence to the status of advanced civilizations—and amicable relations among men.

The market, therefore, is preeminently *social*; and the rest of the *social* consists of other voluntary, friendly, non-market relations, which also, however, are best conducted on the basis of a spiritual *exchange* and mutual gain. (Isn't it better if A and B are *both* friendly to each other, than if A is friendly to B but not vice versa?)

The market, then, far from being a disrupter of society, is society. What, then, would Polanyi use to replace the market? The only relation aside from the voluntary is the coercive; in short, Polanyi would replace the market by the "social" relation of force and violence, of aggression and exploitation. But this is *not* social; it is profoundly *antisocial*. The exploiter, who lives parasitically off the producer by violence, is antisocial, for he is not living according to the best nature of man: by producing and exchanging his produce for the produce of another. He is living by use of violence, one-sidedly and parasitically at the expense of the producer. This is a profoundly antisocial and antihuman relationship. It disrupts the social market and leads it—and with it, civilization and civilized living standards—to crumble into the dust.

Franz Oppenheimer, in his brilliant work, *The State*, put it very well. There are two possible roads to wealth, he wrote: one is by producing, by transforming matter with personal energy, and then exchanging this produce with the produce of another.[87] This he termed the "economic means." Another road is to wait until someone else has produced wealth, and then to seize it by force and violence. This he called the "political means." *Which* method is "social," and which is profoundly and disruptively *anti*social should be easy to see. Karl Polanyi, in claiming to save society *from* the market, is in the process of destroying society

---

[87]Franz Oppenheimer, *The State: Its History and Development Viewed Sociologically*, John M. Gitterman, trans. (New York: Vanguard Press, 1922).

itself by destroying the market. Polanyi's work is an apotheosis of the political means.

That this is what Polanyi will bring should also be evident from his discussion of free labor. For Polanyi, allowing labor to be a "commodity" was one of the worst sins of the free market; Polanyi therefore proposes to take labor out of the free market. But what is the only alternative to free labor? It is *un*free labor, i.e., serfdom. The man who is not allowed to be a free laborer is a serf. In fact, in extolling the process (supposedly typical of the primitive tribe) of *working without pay*, Polanyi is *precisely* extolling the system of *slavery*. For what is unpaid, unfree labor, but slave labor?

Polanyi, like all socialists, is at pains to teach us that the coming of the new "society" without the market is inevitable. Thus, for him, every restriction on the market in the recent century or so came as a "recognition" of social need, and *not* as a deliberate choice governed by certain ideas and interests. To preserve this myth, Polanyi angrily criticizes those, like Mises, who believe that certain definite socialistic and restrictionistic ideas and interests brought about these government interventions in the market. Polanyi sets up a straw man by calling this a "conspiracy" theory of history, which it is not at all.[88] There need be no concerted conspiracy for two different statists or socialists to advocate statist measures in two different fields. (Of course, Polanyi also ignores very important *actual* conspiracies like the Fabians.[89]) The result flows inevitably and "naturally" from the

---

[88]Polanyi writes, "But while we assert that the application of the absurd notion of a self-regulating market system would have inevitably destroyed society, the liberal accuses the most various elements of having wrecked a great initiative." These accusations, in Polanyi's opinion, created "the myth of the anti-liberal conspiracy which in one form or another is common to all liberal interpretations of the events of the 1870s and 1880s." See *The Great Transformation*, pp. 185–86.

[89]In Rothbard's analysis, the Fabians were supposed to have encouraged the birth of imperialism in England at the start of the

premises held by the two men. Not willing to discuss the different and conflicting *ideas* at stake in the problems of socialism versus the market, Polanyi tries to put the whole thing on the plane of social determinism and inevitability, so that human volition plays little or no role in the process.

As a corollary, then, to his rejection of reason, Polanyi also rejects man's free will. Instead, "society" acts, determines, protects, recognizes, etc. In this way the *real* determinants of action in society, the ideas adopted and pursued by individuals, are forgotten, and the spotlight is turned on so-called "social forces," "society," etc.

Like all determinists, Polanyi eventually involves himself in severe contradictions. For, when it comes to the adoption of the *free market* in the nineteenth century, *here*, Polanyi claims, was *not* something socially determined, but the reflection of tragically wrong ideas held by *laissez-faire* ideologues, who by "intervention" in the "natural" (tribal? caste?) processes of state regulation, etc., temporarily brought about a free market.

I could go on almost indefinitely in detailed criticism of Polanyi, but there is no point in prolonging this too much further. That by "society" Polanyi means force and the "political means" is indicated by his repeated warnings that "social reality" necessarily must involve force and violence. (But why not force limited to combating aggressive force, thus minimizing the role of force in society?) Polanyi, in caustically rejecting the ideal of free trade, doesn't realize that he is thereby rejecting international peace, for a world of socialist nations will inevitably conflict with each other's plans, and precipitate conflict of interest and wars.

Also revealing is this quotation:

---

twentieth century. The small group founded by Sidney and Beatrice Webb in 1902, the Coefficients, was said to have the aim, among others, of creating an alliance with Tory imperialism in order to realize Fabian ideas concerning the welfare state. See Murray N. Rothbard, "Left and Right: The Prospects for Liberty," *Left and Right: A Journal of Libertarian Thought* 1 (1965).

> Economic co-operation [in the nineteenth-century free market] was limited to private institutions as rambling and ineffective as free trade, while actual collaboration between peoples, *that is*, between governments, could never even be envisaged.[90]

Note the totalitarian identification of "people" and "government."

Polanyi sees that the commodity money of the old gold standard is indispensable to a true free-market economy, and therefore scornfully denounces it. Like most anti-gold standard, pro-fiat paper men, he at the same time declares that money is *more* than a commodity (more than just a "veil") and much less than a commodity (money is a "mere ticket"): another contradiction.

(Actually, money is a commodity—period.)

Polanyi is also totally wrong when he says that business "needs" continual doses of inflation to bolster purchasing power, which a pure gold standard could not provide, and wrong too when he absurdly maintains that a central bank is not as deflationary, in a contraction, as a pure gold standard without such a central bank. A central bank is inherently more inflationary, but when the day of reckoning comes, and it must contract (under a gold standard), it contracts far more than would otherwise be necessary.

Further, Polanyi seems to think that he has scored a great coup on free-market economists when he says that trade first developed in international and interregional channels, and not first locally and then internationally. So what? This is certainly not in any sense a refutation of free-market economics. It is not surprising that, in a world of self-sufficient farms and manors, the earliest trade should be with far-distant places, which are the only places from which local farms can obtain certain produce (e.g., western Europe could only procure spices from the Near East). This is, in

---

[90]Polanyi, *The Great Transformation*, p. 175; emphasis added.

fact, a *manifestation* of the gains of trade and division of labor, and the growth of the market, and not vice versa.

Finally, in the last chapter, Polanyi tries to assure us that his projected collectivist society would really preserve many of the "freedoms" that, he grudgingly admits, the market economy brought us. This chapter is almost a textbook presentation of utmost confusion about the concept of "freedom"—and of confusion between the vitally distinct concepts of "freedom" and of "power."[91]

Many "freedoms" would be kept, even maximized—after all, isn't a worker with more money more "free," and who cares about the money taken away from the luxurious rich, anyway?— including such "freedom" as the "right to a job" without being discriminated against because of race, creed, or color. Not only does Polanyi vainly think, or assert, that we can have at least *enough* "freedoms" in his collectivist society; he also believes, equally vainly, that we can preserve industrialism and Western civilization.

Both hopes are vain; in both cases, Polanyi thinks he can preserve the *effect* (freedom of speech or industrial civilization), while destroying the *cause* (the free market, private property rights, etc.) In this way, he is thinking not only as Nehru and Kwame Nkrumah think, he is thinking also in the same fashion as the savage whom he so exuberantly extols.

To sum up: I have read few books in my time that have been more vicious or more fallacious.

Murray N. Rothbard

---

[91]Rothbard notes, "On this crucial distinction, always blurred by collectivists, see F.A. von Hayek, *The Road to Serfdom* (London: Routledge, 1944).

CHRONOLOGY OF THE LIFE AND WORKS OF MURRAY NEWTON ROTHBARD

CHRONOLOGY OF THE LIFE AND WORKS OF MURRAY NEWTON ROTHBARD

1926. Murray Newton Rothbard is born in New York on March 2, son of Jewish immigrants from Poland.

1942. Goes to Columbia University and at the end of the Second World War becomes a member of the Young Republican Club of New York. Rothbard is close to the isolationist Old Right, which has, however, lost much of its influence by this time.

1946. Is awarded a master's degree in mathematics.

1949. Attends a seminar on the Austrian School of economics, held by Ludwig von Mises at New York University.

1953. Marries JoAnn Schumaker.

1956. Is awarded a Ph.D. in economics under the guidance of Joseph Dorfman; his thesis is *The Panic of 1819: Reactions and Politics*. In this period he begins to contribute to the journal *Analysis*, edited by Frank Chodorov; to *The Freeman*, the periodical edited by Henry Hazlitt; and to William F. Buckley's *National Review*.

1957. In the *Southern Economic Journal*, publishes the article "In Defense of Extreme Apriorism," a defense of the deductive axiomatic approach of Ludwig von Mises.

1960. Is no longer able to maintain his position at *National Review*, the main American conservative journal. His attacks against the interventionist approach to communism upheld by the editor, William F. Buckley, leads to a split and the end of contributions from Rothbard, who adheres to his consistently antimilitarist position.

1962. *The Panic of 1819* and *Man, Economy, and State* are published. The latter deals with Austrian economics and follows the praxeological method.

1963. Publication of *America's Great Depression*, in which the author applies Mises's business-cycle theory to the years leading up to the economic crisis of 1929 and those immediately afterward. Rothbard maintains that intervention in the fields of credit and industry, resulting from Herbert Hoover's policies, interfered with the capacity of the market to correct its production structure, thus transforming the economic crisis into a long and painful depression.

1965. On April 17, tens of thousands of young people march on Washington, calling for an end to the Vietnam War. Rothbard sympathizes with the youth protest antiwar movement.

1965. Publication of the first issue of the periodical *Left and Right* founded by Rothbard, Leonard Liggio, and George Resch.

1966. Begins to teach at the Polytechnic Institute of New York, where he will stay until 1986.

1968. Briefly joins the Peace and Freedom Party, attempting to find an alliance with the New Left on the basis of criticism of industry/military relations and links with the state. The party has its origins in the youth protest movement. It is soon dissolved.

1969. The Republican youth organization *Young Americans for Freedom* divides on the issues of the Vietnam War and conscription. As a result, a new independent libertarian movement, centered around the Society for Individual Liberty, is born.

1970. Publication of *Power and Market*. It contains a criticism of philosophical arguments against the market and an exposition of the anarcho-capitalist theory of private protection agencies.

1972. The Libertarian Party is founded.

1973. Rothbard joins the Libertarian Party and publishes *For a New Liberty: The Libertarian Manifesto*. The volume is intended as a guide to modern libertarianism. The author identifies a long list of problematic areas related to state activities, proposing a free-market solution for each. He supports the private provision of security, both internal and external, and the private supply of all judicial services.

1977. The Cato Institute, a libertarian think tank founded by Charles Koch with Rothbard's collaboration, establishes its headquarters in San Francisco. At Rothbard's instigation, the institute founds reviews such as *Libertarian Review*, the *Journal of Libertarian Studies*, and *Inquiry*. At the end of the 1970s, relations between Rothbard and the Cato Institute begin to deteriorate. Ed Crane, representing Koch, opts for a decidedly less radical line than Rothbard's. The headquarters moves to Washington, D.C., and Cato becomes a conservative think tank. Rothbard leaves the institute.

1975–1978. Publication of the four-volume *Conceived in Liberty*, a libertarian history of the American colonies from the sixteenth century up to the War of Independence. In the experiences of the American colonies, Rothbard recognizes the progress of the libertarian idea, culminating in the Declaration of Independence, an act of rebellion against the British government.

1982. Llewellyn H. Rockwell founds the Ludwig von Mises Institute with the support of Mises's widow, Margit. Rothbard accepts the position of vice president. The partnership with the Mises Institute and with Rockwell will last for the rest of his life. *The Ethics of Liberty* is published. This work is an attempt on Rothbard's part to base the market economy on the theory of natural law.

1985. Appointed to the position of S.J. Hall Distinguished Professor of Economics at the University of Nevada at Las Vegas.

1995. Dies in New York on January 7. Two volumes of *An Austrian Perspective on the History of Economic Thought* are published posthumously.

REFERENCES AND BIBLIOGRAPHY

References[1]

Buckley, William F. *God and Man at Yale: The Superstitions of Academic Freedom*. Chicago: Regnery, 1951.

Carmichael, Leonard. "Absolutes, Relativism and the Scientific Psychology of Human Nature." In H. Schoeck and J. W. Wiggins, eds., *Relativism and the Study of Man*. Princeton, N.J.: D. Van Nostrand, 1961.

Cutten, George B. "Rugged Individualism." *Vital Speeches of the Day* (November 5, 1934).

Hayek, Friedrich A. von. *The Road to Serfdom*. Chicago: Chicago University Press, 1944.

———. *The Constitution of Liberty*. Chicago: University of Chicago Press, 1960.

Juvenal, *Satires VI*.

Leoni, Bruno. "Some Reflections on the 'Relativistic' Meaning of the *Wertfreiheit* in the Study of Man." In H. Schoeck and J. W. Wiggins, eds., *Relativism and the Study of Man*. Princeton, N.J.: D. Van Nostrand, 1961.

Mises, Ludwig von. "Epistemological Relativism in the Sciences of Human Action." In H. Schoeck and J. W. Wiggins, eds., *Relativism and the Study of Man*. Princeton, N.J.: D. Van Nostrand, 1961.

Nock, Albert J. *Our Enemy the State*. New York: William Morrow, 1935.

---

[1]Books and articles that Rothbard references in his correspondance with the Volker Fund.

Oppenheimer, Franz. *The State: Its History and Development Viewed Sociologically*, trans. John M. Gitterman. New York: Vanguard Press, 1922.

Paterson, Isabel. *The God of the Machine.* New York: Putnam, 1943.

Polanyi, Karl. *The Great Transformation.* New York: Holt, Rinehart, and Winston, 1944.

Robbins, Caroline. *The Eighteenth Century Commonwealthman: Studies in the Transmission, Development, and Circumstance of English Liberal Thought from the Restoration of Charles II until the War with the Thirteen Colonies.* Cambridge, Mass.: Harvard University Press, 1959.

Robbins, Lionel. *The Great Depression.* London: Macmillan, 1934.

Schoeck, Helmut and James W. Wiggins, eds. *Relativism and the Study of Man.* Princeton, N.J.: D. Van Nostrand, 1961.

Stanlis, Peter. *Edmund Burke and the Natural Law.* Ann Arbor: University of Michigan Press, 1958.

Strauss, Leo. *On Tyranny: An Interpretation of Xenophon's "Hiero."* London: Political Science Classics, 1948.

———. *Thoughts on Machiavelli.* Glencoe, Ill.: Free Press, 1958.

———. *What is Political Philosophy? And Other Studies.* Glencoe, Ill.: Free Press, 1959.

———. "Relativism." In H. Schoeck and J. W. Wiggins, eds., *Relativism and the Study of Man.* Princeton, N.J.: D. Van Nostrand, 1961.

Vivas, Eliseo. "Reiterations and Second Thoughts on Cultural Relativism." In H. Schoeck and J. W. Wiggins, eds., *Relativism and the Study of Man.* Princeton, N.J.: D. Van Nostrand, 1961.

Wild, John. *Plato's Modern Enemies and the Theory of Natural Law.* Chicago: University of Chicago Press, 1953.

Wittfogel, Karl August. *Oriental Despotism.* New Haven, Conn.: Yale University Press, 1957.

BIBLIOGRAPHY

Selected Writings by Murray N. Rothbard

The Panic of 1819. New York: Columbia University Press, 1962.

Man, Economy, and State. Princeton, N.J.: D. Van Nostrand, 1962.

"On 'Freedom and the Law'." *New Individualist Review* 1, no. 4 (1962).

America's Great Depression. Princeton, N.J.: D. Van Nostrand, 1963.

"Left and Right: the Prospects for Liberty." *Left and Right: A Journal of Libertarian Thought* 1 (1965).

Power and Market. Menlo Park, N.J.: Institute for Humane Studies, 1970.

For a New Liberty: The Libertarian Manifesto. New York: MacMillan, 1973.

Individualism and the Philosophy of Social Sciences. San Francisco: Cato Institute, 1979.

"Hayek on Coercion and Freedom." *Literature of Liberty* 3, no. 4 (1980).

The Ethics of Liberty. Atlantic Highlands, N.J.: Humanities Press, 1982.

An Austrian Perspective on the History of Economic Thought. Vol. I, *Economic Thought Before Adam Smith*. Cheltenham: Edward Elgar, 1995.

An Austrian Perspective on the History of Economic Thought. Vol. II, *Classical Economics*. Cheltenham: Edward Elgar, 1995.

"The Present State of Austrian Economics." In *The Logic of Action I: Method, Money and the Austrian School*. Cheltenham: Edward Elgar, 1997.

Writings on Murray N. Rothbard

Barry, Norman P. *On Classical Liberalism and Libertarianism.* London: Macmillan, 1986.

——. "Rothbard's Liberty, Economy and State." *Journal des économistes et des études humaines* 6 (March 1995).

Bassani, Luigi Marco. "L'anarco-capitalismo di Murray Newton Rothbard." Introduction to *L'etica della libertà*, by Murray N. Rothbard, pp. xi–xliv. Macerata: Liberilibri, 1996.

Block, Walter and Llewellyn H. Rockwell, eds. *Man, Economy, and Liberty: Essays in Honor of Murray N. Rothbard.* Auburn, Ala.: Ludwig von Mises Institute, 1988.

Cubeddu, Raimondo. "Murray N. Rothbard." In *Enciclopedia del pensiero politico.* Roma-Bari: Laterza, 2000.

Gordon, David. *Murray N. Rothbard: A Scholar in Defense of Freedom: A Bibliographical Essay.* Auburn, Ala.: Ludwig von Mises Institute, 1986.

Iannello, N. "Concepite in libertà: Le nazioni libertarie nel modello di Murray Rothbard." In *Nazione cos'è*, edited by N. Iannello and C. Lottieri. Treviglio: L. Flacco Editore, 1996.

Lottieri, C. "Anarchici per il capitalismo." *Ideazione* no. 5 (1996).

Mazzone, Stefania. *Stato e anarchia: Il pensiero politico del libertarismo americano.* Milan: Giuffrè, 2000.

Modugno, Roberta A. *Murray N. Rothbard e l'anarco-capitalismo americano.* Soveria Mannelli: Rubbettino, 1998.

——. "La teoria politica anarco-capitalista di Murray N. Rothbard nel suo contesto storico e intellettuale." *Nuova civiltà delle macchine* 16, no. 3–4 (1998).

——. "Introduzione a La libertà dei libertari." In *Antologia di scritti di Murray N. Rothbard.* Soveria Mannelli: Rubbettino, 2000.

——. "L'anarco-capitalismo di Murray N. Rothbard: Fonti e dibattito contemporaneo." In *Individualismo metodologico: dalla Scuola austriaca all'anarco-capitalismo*, edited by

David Gordon and Roberta A. Modugno. Rome: Luiss Edizioni, 2001.

Raimondo, Justin. *An Enemy of the State: The Life of Murray N. Rothbard.* New York: Prometheus Books, 2000.

Writings of a General Nature

Antiseri, Dario. *Liberi perché fallibili.* Soveria Mannelli: Rubbettino, 1995.

———. *Trattato di metodologia delle scienze sociali.* Turin: UTET, 2000.

Antiseri, Dario, Giovanni Fornero, and Franco Restaino. *La filosofia contemporanea.* Vol. 4 of *Storia della Filosofia,* edited by Nicola Abbagnano. Turin: UTET, 2003.

Bobbio, Norberto. *L'età dei diritti.* Turin: Einaudi, 1997.

Cubeddu, Raimondo. *Atlante del liberalismo.* Rome: Ideazione, 1997.

———. *Legge naturale o diritti naturali? Alcune questioni di filosofia politica liberale.* Rome: Quaderni dell'Istituto Acton, 2004.

Drury, Shadia. *The Political Ideas of Leo Strauss.* New York: St. Martin's Press, 1988.

Fassò, Guido. *La legge della ragione.* Milan: Giuffrè, 1999.

Finnis, John. *Natural Law and Natural Rights.* Oxford: Clarendon Press, 1980.

Foot, Philippa. *Virtues and Vices.* Berkeley: University of California Press, 1978.

———. *Natural Goodness.* Oxford: Clarendon Press, 2001.

Hamowy, Ronald. "Hayek's Concept of Freedom: A Critique." *New Individualist Review* 1, no. 1 (1961).

———. "Freedom and the Rule of Law in F.A. Hayek." *Il politico* (1971–1972).

———. "Law and the Liberal Society: F.A. Hayek's *Constitution of Liberty.*" *Journal of Libertarian Studies* 2, no. 4 (1978).

Hayek, Friedrich A. *Individualism: True and False.* London: Routledge and Kegan Paul, 1949.

——. *The Counter Revolution of Science: Studies in the Abuse of Reason.* Glencoe, Ill.: The Free Press, 1952.

——. *The Constitution of Liberty.* Chicago: University of Chicago Press, 1960.

——. *Studies in Philosophy, Politics and Economics.* London: Routledge and Kegan Paul, 1967.

——. *Law, Legislation and Liberty.* London: Routledge, 1982.

——. *The Fatal Conceit.* London: Routledge, 1988.

Leoni, Bruno. *La libertà e la legge.* Macerata: Liberilibri, 1994.

Lottieri, Carlo. *Il pensiero libertario contemporaneo.* Macerata: Liberilibri, 2001.

Matteucci, Nicola. *Lo Stato moderno.* Bologna: Il Mulino, 1997.

Mises, Ludwig von. *Human Action* (1949). Auburn, Ala.: Ludwig von Mises Institute, 1998.

Noto, Sergio, ed. *Alessandro Passerin d'Entreves pensatore europeo.* Bologna: Il Mulino, 2004.

Passerin d'Entrèves, Alessandro. *La dottrina del diritto naturale.* Milan: Edizioni di Comunità, 1954.

Popper, Karl R. *The Poverty of Historicism.* Boston: Beacon Press, 1957.

Raico, Ralph. "La tradizione liberale francese dell'Ottocento." *Federalismo e libertà*, no. 5–6 (2001).

Schoeck, Helmut and James W. Wiggins, eds. *Relativism and the Study of Man.* Princeton, N.J.: D. Van Nostrand, 1961.

Sciabarra, Chris Matthew. *Total Freedom: Toward a Dialectical Libertarianism.* University Park: Pennsylvania State University Press, 2000.

Strauss, Leo. *Natural Right and History.* Chicago: University of Chicago Press, 1950.

——. *Gerusalemme e Atene: Studi sul pensiero politico dell'Occidente.* Turin: Einaudi, 1998. Translation of a lecture given at the City College of New York in 1967, titled "Jer-susalem and Athens: Some Preliminary Reflections."

Tierney, Brian. *The Idea of Natural Rights: Studies on Natural Rights, Natural Law, and Church Law 1150–1625.* Atlanta, Ga.: Scholars Press, 1997.

Vaughn, Karen I. *Austrian Economics in America: The Migration of a Tradition.* Cambridge: Cambridge University Press, 1994.

Veatch, Henry B. *Human Rights: Fact or Fancy?* Baton Rouge: Louisiana State University Press, 1985.

Vernaglione, Piero. *Il libertarismo.* Soveria Mannelli: Rubbettino, 2003.

Villey, Michel. *La formation de la pensée juridique moderne.* Paris: Editions Montchrestien, 1975.

Zanotto, Paolo. *Il movimento libertario Americano dagli anni sessanta ad oggi: radici storico- dottrinali e discriminanti ideologico politiche.* Siena: Di. Gips. Università di Siena, 2001. Reprinted in *Alessandro Passerin d'Entrèves pensatore europeo,* edited by Sergio Noto. Bologna: Il Mulino, 2004.

INDEX

Index